JB
Pier

Hm 9913

Brown, Fern G.

Franklin Pierce.

Franklin Pierce

14th President of the United States

A handsome man of high principles, Franklin Pierce was a President who stood for states' rights on the eve of the Civil War. During Pierce's term in the White House, he did his best to hold the country together and preserve the Union. (Smithsonian Institution Photo No. 21364-K.)

Franklin Pierce
14th President of the United States

Fern G. Brown

9913
17.26

GARRETT EDUCATIONAL CORPORATION

Manufactured in the United States of America

Edited and produced by Synthegraphics Corporation

Library of Congress Cataloging in Publication Data

Brown, Fern G.
  Franklin Pierce, 14th president of the United States / Fern G. Brown.
  (Presidents of the United States)
  Bibliography: p.
  Includes index.
  Summary: A biography of the New Hampshire politician who served as president during a period of increasing bitterness between the North and the South.
  1. Pierce, Franklin, 1804–1869 – Juvenile literature.
2. Presidents – United States – Biography – Juvenile literature. 3. Pierce, Franklin, 1804–1869. [1. Presidents.] I. Title. II. Title: Franklin Pierce, fourteenth president of the United States. III. Series.
E432.B854   1989   973.6'6'0924 – dc19   [B]   [92]
88-30050
ISBN 0-944483-25-9

Contents

Chronology for Franklin Pierce

1804 Born on November 23 in Hillsboro, New Hampshire

1820– 1824 Attended Bowdoin College in Brunswick, Maine

1827 Admitted to the New Hampshire bar

1828 Elected moderator of Hillsborough, New Hampshire, town meeting

1829– 1832 Member of New Hampshire legislature; elected speaker in 1831

1832– 1837 Member of U.S. House of Representatives

1834 Married Jane Means Appleton on November 19

1837– 1842 Served as a U.S. Senator; resigned from Senate and became chairman of the State Central Committee of the Democratic Party

1844 Reappointed state chairman of the Democratic Party

1845 Appointed federal district attorney for New Hampshire by President Polk

1847– 1848 First appointed a colonel then a brigadier general in Mexican-American War

1850 Elected chairman of New Hampshire Constitutional Convention

1853– 1857 Served as 14th President of the United States

1869 Died on October 8

Chapter 1

The Youngest President

It was a warm April day in 1852. Franklin Pierce was in the study of his home in Concord, New Hampshire, reading an exciting letter. His friend, Benjamin French, had written to ask if he wanted to be the next President of the United States! Pierce was flattered. He had retired from Congress years before, vowing that he was finished serving his country in public office. Yet he had mixed emotions about running for President now. What should his answer be?

THE RELUCTANT CANDIDATE

Besides having been designated New Hampshire's "favorite son" in the upcoming presidential election, Pierce had not been very involved in national politics. He knew that favorite son status was just a friendly gesture. He did not think there was the slightest chance that he would be nominated at the Democratic National Convention.

Pierce picked up his quill pen. He was not anxious to be President. To his mind, living in Washington had many disadvantages. Yet, his party might need him. Perhaps by being President, he thought, he could bring glory to his home

1

state. Finally, he wrote to French that he would leave the matter in the hands of his friends in Washington to decide "what is my duty and what may be in the best interest of the party."

That year, the Democratic National Convention was to begin on June 1 in Baltimore, Maryland. Lewis Cass of Michigan, William Marcy of New York, James Buchanan of Pennsylvania, and Stephen A. Douglas of Illinois were the leading Democratic contenders for the presidential nomination. But speaking out on the problems of the day had made each of the four major candidates many enemies, and there was much bitterness and rivalry between them.

Pierce's friends in Washington worked undercover mentioning his name as a possibility for President whenever they could. Although he was a powerful Democrat in New Hampshire, he was not a well-known national figure. But because he had served in the U.S. House of Representatives, in the Senate, and had few enemies, his chances of being nominated were fairly good.

Pierce met with his supporters, and they urged him to announce his candidacy, but he was stubborn. He would not run unless the Democratic Party could not agree on one of the four other announced candidates. If there was a deadlock, he was willing to be the compromise candidate.

A Deadlocked Convention

At convention time, Pierce was at his home in Concord awaiting news by telegram from Baltimore. He finally received word that 17 ballots had been cast, but no candidate had been chosen as yet. Excitement was mounting!

The next day there were 16 more ballots; 33 in all so far! That evening, when the delegates adjourned, it seemed to everyone that Lewis Cass had the most votes and would be nominated in the morning. Pierce was so sure Cass would get the nomination that he and his wife Jane went to Boston. He was happy to escape from the half-wanted, half-feared success of being nominated. The tenseness of the last few days — waiting for the telegrams to come, waiting for the results of ballot after ballot — had been exhausting.

The following morning, Mr. and Mrs. Pierce went for a carriage ride. They were heading back to Boston when they saw a horseman galloping toward them at breakneck speed. Waving wildly, he was yelling something at the top of his voice. Finally coming abreast of the carriage, he tugged at his horse's reins and shouted breathlessly, "Mr. Pierce! The convention has nominated you!"

Pierce could not believe his ears. Mrs. Pierce fainted when she heard the news. He had been nominated to run for President by the Democratic Party on the 49th ballot! In the fall of 1852, Franklin Pierce, at the age of 48, the youngest presidential candidate up to that time — the man who had been reluctant to run — was elected the 14th President of the United States.

GROWING UP IN NEW HAMPSHIRE

The first American ancestor of Franklin Pierce on record was Thomas Pierce. He left England in 1634 when he was a young man and came to America in search of religious freedom, settling in Charlestown, Massachusetts. Franklin was seventh in the American line started by Thomas Pierce.

Franklin's father, named Benjamin, was born in Chelmsford, Massachusetts, in 1757. One April day, when Benjamin Pierce was 18 years old, word reached him while plowing a field that the British had killed eight Americans at Lexington. Angrily, Benjamin unwrapped the reins of the plow and unyoked the oxen. Grabbing his uncle's fowling piece (a light shotgun used for shooting birds), he took a bullet pouch and powder horn and enlisted in the Continental Army.

After the Revolutionary War, Benjamin Pierce bought a 50-acre farm on a branch of the Contoocook River in Hillsboro County (later Hillsborough), New Hampshire. In 1787, he married Elizabeth Andrews, who died in childbirth, leaving a daughter named Elizabeth but who was called Betsy. Two years later, Benjamin married Anna Kendrick, a highstrung, pretty woman who was the daughter of a local businessman and farmer. They had eight children: Benjamin, Nancy, John Sullivan, Harriet, Charles Grandison, Franklin, Charlotte, and Henry Dearborn.

Franklin was his mother's favorite child, and he adored her. He looked very much like his mother, and they seemed to have similar personalities. Of his mother, Franklin later wrote: "She was a most affectionate and tender mother, strong in many points, and weak in some, but always weak on the side of kindness and deep affection."

Backcountry Life

Franklin Pierce was born on November 23, 1804, in the Pierces' log cabin on the Contoocook River. Shortly after his birth, the family moved from the isolated farm to a much larger home in Hillsborough Lower Village.

Franklin, a good-looking boy with blue eyes and light curly hair, had a gentle disposition. He was healthy, athletic, and he especially liked to fish and hunt. Because many friends and relatives from Massachusetts bought farms nearby, Franklin always had lots of companions.

The Pierce household was a noisy and lively place. Their home, which was on a highway, was also an inn and tavern. When stagecoaches from Keene, Dunstable, or Concord came by, travelers would often stop in for refreshments, sometimes

Franklin Pierce was born in a log cabin in Hillsboro, New Hampshire. The home shown here, which was not far from Pierce's birthplace, is the one to which his family moved when he was six weeks old. This is where Pierce spent his boyhood years. (Library of Congress.)

staying overnight. The travelers brought the Pierce family news of the world. Eagerly, Franklin listened to tales of the new nation growing up around him. Hillsborough was only six hours by horseback from Concord, the state capital, but to the young boy, it seemed very far away.

Franklin's father wanted to give his children a good education. Young Franklin was taught to read, write, and do arithmetic. He was a good pupil, one of two in the family who really wanted to learn. Combined with Franklin's desire to learn was his reverence for military life, encouraged by the heroic Revolutionary War stories told him by his father and his father's friends. His father, now a general in the state militia (a defense force made up of local citizens), was Franklin's role model. If anyone asked Franklin what he wanted to be when he grew up, he would say, "A soldier in command of battalions."

The War of 1812 with Great Britain came home to the Pierce family when the oldest son, Benjamin, left school to join the Army. John McNeil, the husband of Franklin's older sister, Betsy, also became a soldier, as did another brother, John. Being too young to fight, Franklin was sent to the local school instead.

Hancock Academy

For a while, Franklin attended a one-room schoolhouse at Hillsborough Center, 1½ miles from home. Then, when he was 12, he was sent to Hancock Academy, a boarding school that was a few miles farther away. Franklin was terribly homesick at Hancock and one Sunday decided that he had had enough of school. He slipped out and walked all the way home. When he arrived, everyone was at church, so he sat down to wait, afraid of what his father might do when he saw him.

When General Pierce came home, he quietly greeted his son and invited him to join the family for dinner. Seated at the table with his parents, brothers, and sisters, Franklin breathed easier. Because it was lonely at boarding school, he was much happier being home.

After dinner, when General Pierce had the carriage hitched up, Franklin realized that he would not be staying home. Instead, he was being taken back to school, but not all the way back. After traveling halfway, his father ordered Franklin to leave the carriage and walk the rest of the way. Although he did not like Hancock Academy, Franklin never ran away from school again. The general's obedience lesson stayed with Franklin all of his life.

COLLEGE DAYS

After his early schooling at Hancock Academy, Franklin attended Francestown and Exeter Academies to prepare for college. He earned the reputation of being a happy-go-lucky, practical joker whose pranks and fights often got him into trouble. Social life, rather than study, occupied his time, yet he managed to complete the work he needed to enter college.

Franklin's father selected Bowdoin College in Brunswick, Maine, because Dr. William Allen, the president, held the same political views that he did. Both men believed in strong states' rights and a minimum of federal authority. Franklin's brother, Benjamin, had attended Dartmouth College, but Dartmouth was now led by Federalist Party thinkers. This was the party of Washington, John Adams, and others who believed in a strong federal government. Franklin's father thought the Federalists were as bad as the British he had fought against in the Revolutionary War.

In September of 1820, Franklin, now a small, slight, 16-

year-old boy, was brought to Bowdoin College by his parents. After passing his entrance exams at President Allen's home, Franklin became one of 19 students in the class of 1824.

On His Own

College life was strict in those days, and there were many rules. Supposedly, students were there to learn, and no nonsense was tolerated. Tuition was $24 a year, and room and board were around two dollars a week.

The Bowdoin campus was little more than a clearing in the pine woods. There were only three buildings: Maine Hall, the student center where the upperclassmen lived and attended classes; Massachusetts Hall, which was the science building; and the chapel. The chapel, an unpainted, unheated wooden building, also housed the library, which was open for one hour a day. Freshmen were only allowed to borrow one book every three weeks!

Franklin's parents thought that he would change his study habits and work harder in college. But during his freshman year, he studied his Latin, Greek, and arithmetic as little as possible. He liked his newfound freedom. Many hours were spent alone wandering in the woods, shooting pigeons, picking blueberries, swimming, fishing, and just plain daydreaming. Franklin also made several visits to a local fortune teller, who foretold his future in tea leaves and cards. And the outgoing, fun-loving youth was even known to frequent a nearby tavern that was off limits to Bowdoin College students.

Lifelong Friends

To Franklin Pierce, the real value of attending college was in the friends he made. At the start of his second year, while going back to school by stagecoach, he met three incoming freshmen. Among them was a shy fellow named Nathaniel Hawthorne. Pierce and Hawthorne liked each other the moment they met, and they became lifelong friends. Hawthorne, who later became Pierce's biographer, was a quiet, compassionate young man with a questioning mind. Through their friendship, Pierce learned some of these qualities, giving him a sensitivity to people and problems that helped him as President.

Zenas Caldwell was another Bowdoin student who became an intimate friend of Franklin's. Several years older, he was a devout Methodist who later became a famous and powerful preacher. Caldwell, too, was a strong influence on Franklin's life.

During Franklin's sophomore year, logic, algebra, and geometry were added to his Greek and Latin classes, but he still did not bother to study very much. Carefree and irresponsible, Franklin devoted most of his time to having fun. Instead of doing his assignments, he copied them from others.

One day, when his algebra teacher called on him, Franklin had correctly solved a difficult problem. The surprised teacher, knowing that Franklin usually did not study very hard, asked him how he got the answer. Without hesitation, Franklin replied, "From Stowe's slate." Franklin may have been irresponsible, but he was honest, which was one of his leading characteristics.

A New Leaf

Early in his junior year, when class standings were posted, young Pierce found that he was the lowest man in his class. It made him so embarrassed and furious that he would not attend lectures for several days. Caldwell prayed for him, and Hawthorne encouraged him to pull himself together and start studying.

Franklin tried to study but could not concentrate. It was difficult for him to cultivate good work habits when he had neglected his studies for so long. Then Caldwell appointed him to be a chapel monitor to help with chapel services. By having to attend chapel every day, Franklin became a changed person. He proved he could accept responsibility. He never again missed a lecture and always came to class prepared. As a result, his grades began to improve. By the summer of 1824, at the end of Franklin's senior year, he stood third in his class.

When commencement approached, Franklin was overjoyed to be asked to give one of the graduating speeches. His first thought was of how proud his father would be. But much to his regret, when Franklin was graduated from Bowdoin College, his father and family could not be there to share the happy occasion.

Chapter 2
Law and Politics

In April 1828, Franklin Pierce was riding his horse to Amherst, New Hampshire. He was on his way to court to try his first case. For any young lawyer, the first appearance in court is an important event, but for Pierce it was even more so. Since he had gone into law, he had not had many clients, and he was afraid that people did not think he was a good lawyer. He had worked extremely hard all winter to prepare this case, and he was determined to prove that he was competent.

But much to his disappointment, Pierce lost the case. However, he did not sit around and mope for days, as he had done in college when he was the lowest man in his class. Instead, he told a friend who tried to console him, ". . . I will try nine hundred and ninety-nine cases, if clients will continue to trust me, and if I fail just as I have today, will try the thousandth." For Franklin Pierce, his failure made him even more determined to become a success at law, and it was not long before he began to win a few cases.

BECOMING A LAWYER

When Franklin Pierce was graduated from Bowdoin in 1824, James Monroe was finishing his second term as the fifth President of the United States. The years Monroe was in office were called "the Era of Good Feeling," because the Federalist Party had almost completely died out, and the majority of politicians were Democratic-Republicans. There were still political differences in the new nation, but the differences were within the party itself.

Young Pierce would have liked to join the Army after graduation. But because the country was not at war, his services were not needed by the military. College had trained him for public life. Yet, if he was to become a politician like his father, who was deeply involved in New Hampshire politics, he would have to learn more about the nation's laws. Since politics did not pay much in those days, politicians often became lawyers to earn a living, and law seemed to be a good field for Pierce.

Champions of the People

The law profession at that time was made up of many different activities. Lawyers not only pleaded cases in court, they were also thought of as champions of the people. Those who wanted to become lawyers studied law books, federal and state constitutions, and they learned about the American political system by holding various offices. In addition, most of them were polished orators. Their resonant, fiery, and sometimes flowery voices would fire up and stimulate an audience.

In 1824 everyone in a town or village knew everyone else, and they thought of politicians as leaders in public affairs. Politicians worked for the good of the community, and many of them sought power as the reward for their work instead of money.

When Franklin came home from Bowdoin, his father held the office of postmaster of Hillsborough, a position for which he was paid. The general gave the job to Franklin, who sold stamps and delivered the mail on horseback while studying law under a local lawyer.

That fall, the Pierces' hero, Andrew Jackson, the leader of the Democratic-Republican Party, was running for President against a large field of candidates that included Henry Clay, William H. Crawford, and John Quincy Adams. General Pierce still thought of Adams as a despised Federalist and did not trust him, nor did he like the other men. Jackson was his man, and he said so loud and clear.

There was so much political activity going on at his father's home that Franklin found it impossible to concentrate on his law studies. So, in the spring of 1825, he went to Portsmouth, New Hampshire, to study in the law office of Levi Woodbury, a family friend. During his first few months there, Franklin studied every day from early in the morning until late at night. He hardly ever went out. For the man who had led such a busy social life in college, it was quite a change.

After completing his law studies in September 1827, Franklin was admitted to the New Hampshire bar (able to practice law in the state). His father built him an office across the road from their home and paid half of the $50.75 it cost for a 75-volume law library. Franklin Pierce, the lawyer, was in business.

An Up-and-Coming Politician

However, it was politics and the Democratic-Republican cause, rather than the law, that soon occupied Franklin's time. Young Pierce led the parade when friends of Andrew Jackson gathered to celebrate the anniversary of their hero's victory over the British at New Orleans at the end of the War of 1812. At the banquet that evening, Franklin's speech was enthusiastically applauded.

Franklin's father was now considered to be the most influential man in New Hampshire politics. In 1827 he was elected governor. Because of his father's influence, Franklin's rise in local and state politics was quick and easy. In 1828 he was elected moderator (chairman) of the Hillsborough town meeting and served in that capacity for six consecutive years. Franklin loved the sociability of politics and his growing status, yet the money he made was not nearly enough for the amount of time and effort he put in.

By this time, the "Era of Good Feeling" was just a memory, and the infighting between the supporters of Adams and Jackson led to many bitter political arguments. During this period, his involvement in politics brought more law business to Franklin Pierce. In the month of January 1828, Franklin had as much business as he had had in the entire six months previously. The following May, he was appointed justice of the peace and received a salary. In 1829 the people of Hillsborough elected him to be their representative at the state legislature in Concord to serve for four years.

THE GOVERNOR'S SON

Out of the New Hampshire backcountry came newly elected Franklin Pierce, only 24 years old. Although his father had lost his bid for a second term as governor, Franklin did serve during the last few months of his father's term. Franklin is the only man in New Hampshire's history to serve in the state legislature while his father served as governor. Representing 2,000 of his townsmen as a state legislator, young Franklin's political career was now launched in the city of Concord.

Concord was a quiet little town of less than 4,000 people that came alive to welcome the 239 lawmakers whenever the state legislature—the Great and General Court—was in session. The first week of the legislature was known as election week, and it was a time of great celebration.

Visitors poured in from nearby towns, and Concord took on a noisy, circus-like atmosphere. There were peddlers, showmen, and refreshment booths lining Main Street, all selling food and drink, apples, gingerbread, and candy. Plenty of wine, whiskey, and New England rum were laid out in the shade. Most of the backwoods representatives were rough, hard-drinking men, and Franklin would sometimes join them and drink more than he should.

Committee Chairman

Usually, first-term lawmakers did not rate much notice in the state legislature. But all eyes were on the governor's son. Although Franklin had resolved to sit and listen at first, his colleagues would not let him. Despite his youth and inexperience, he was made chairman of the Committee on Education because he had been to college.

As chairman, Franklin led an investigation into the management of primary education in the state. The question was: Should education be managed by a general committee from each town, or by committees in the school districts into which each town was divided? Legislator Pierce and his committee decided that if education was managed by the school districts, it would be more representative of the people.

Franklin made his first speech in the legislature on the subject of newspaper publishing. At that time, the state paid the newspapers for publishing the laws the legislature had passed, considering it the same as advertising. Because most of the papers were anti-Jackson, young Pierce wanted to publish the new state laws only in papers that were pro-Jackson. Many others spoke for and against this bill, but it was Pierce's speech that helped the most to pass the measure.

This speech tells us a great deal about Franklin Pierce. He claimed to stand on high principles, but in this case, it was politics, pure and simple: Franklin wanted the government business to go only to those newspapers that were on his side. From then on, Pierce always managed to find a high principle to back his practical political ideas.

Learning Party Organization

Besides attending legislative sessions, Franklin also made himself popular with the Jacksonian Democrats. Every evening he would meet with them at the Eagle Coffee Shop, where they would discuss politics and make plans to beat their enemies. A smart political student, Franklin quickly learned about party organization, often called a "political machine," and how the machine "bosses" controlled legislation.

One important tool of a political machine is the "caucus," a closed meeting of political party members making policy decisions and selecting candidates for office. It was at such caucuses that the Jacksonians decided to gradually drop the name Democratic-Republicans; they would eventually become the Democratic Party.

Franklin was also present at many caucuses held by the Jacksonians in the so-called "Dictator's Palace." The room next to the office of Isaac Hill, the well-known newspaper editor of the *Patriot,* had earned that name from the opposition press because Hill was an important advisor to President Jackson. For Franklin, his first experiences with a caucus set within an enthusiastic party organization made public service and party loyalty seem to him to be one and the same.

FINDING A PLACE

When Franklin's first legislative session was over, he and his father returned to Hillsborough. But now Franklin was bored going from house to office every day, just barely making a living at law. He missed the excitement of Concord and hated being stuck in the backwoods with no social life. Because he did not feel much like working, he did some traveling on family matters. But New Year's Day of 1830 found him depressed by the boredom of his life.

General Pierce's term as governor expired that year, and because he was in his seventies, he decided to retire from politics. After the old general was honored for his years of service by the people of Hillsborough, they turned to his son to carry on the family's political tradition. At the annual town meeting, Franklin was chosen moderator for the third time and was again selected as the town's legislator. As winter turned to spring, Franklin's mood lifted, and he looked forward to going back to Concord for the next session of the state legislature.

The Jacksonians were still in power when Franklin returned to Concord in the spring of 1830. During this session of the state legislature, he was made chairman of the Committee on Towns and Parishes and he learned about "gerrymandering" (moving political boundaries in order to influence an election). This gave him even more experience in the give and take of practical politics.

During the winter between the 1830 and 1831 legislative sessions, Franklin was more active in his law practice and less moody. He was in good health and happy that he was at last achieving some success in his law work.

Speaker of the House

In 1831 Franklin was once again sent back to the state legislature, where he was elected speaker of the House. Because he was only 26 years old, he doubted whether he had enough experience to preside over 229 legislators. But when he took over the speaker's duties, he proved to be very much in control.

Benjamin French said Pierce was a "devilish fine speaker" whom everyone liked. Nathaniel Hawthorne wrote that he saw a development of his friend's mind and that Franklin now had a greater power to influence other men. "He had all the natural gifts that adapted him for the post of speaker: courtesy, firmness, quickness and accuracy of judgment and a clearness of mental perception that brought its own regularity into the scene of confused and entangled debate."

Franklin was a handsome figure in his frock coat and big tie as he presided over the legislature. He enjoyed the excitement of the debates and the airing of opposing views. That year, too, he was appointed a military aide by Governor Samuel Dinsmoor and received the honorary title of colonel. When anybody called him "Colonel Pierce," it brought back memories of his boyhood and the stories told to him by his father's friends about glorious Revolutionary War battles.

Chapter 3

The Young Congressman

In the spring of 1832, when the news reached Hillsborough that Andrew Jackson had been renominated to run for President, fun-loving Franklin Pierce and his friends wanted to celebrate the happy event. But the way they celebrated almost caused Franklin's death. They found an old cannon that had not been used since the Revolutionary War and tried to fire it. The cannon's carriage was gone, but the long metal tube was still there. They needed a gun carriage, but they could not find one.

Then someone came up with the idea to mount the cannon on a pair of wooden cart wheels and an axle. They chained the gun to the axle and lugged it to the top of Meeting House Hill, where the townspeople celebrated all patriotic events. The young Jacksonians figured that the renomination of their chief was as patriotic an event as there could be.

The Revolutionary War cannon worked like all cannons do; when it was fired, it kicked backwards violently. To account for the kickback, the old cannons were mounted on slides. Then, when they were fired, the guns would slide back and not go out of control. But because Franklin and his friends had chained their gun to the axle, it could not slide back when they fired it. Instead, there was an enormous roar, a thick, black cloud of smoke filled the sky, and the cannon jumped backwards. Frantically, the men leaped out of the way. Franklin was lucky that he was not hurt or killed by the cannon.

CONGRESSMAN PIERCE

When Jackson was nominated for re-election in 1832, there was not much opposition. New Hampshire was behind the President 100 percent. Pierce was also returned to Concord that year as a representative from Hillsborough and was re-elected speaker by a vote of 297 to 3.

Because he now received $2.50 a day for expenses, Speaker Pierce could afford to stay at a local hotel. He cheerfully paid the extravagant price of one dollar a day for room and board. Furthermore, there were additional charges on his bill for such extras as wine, cigars, and board for his horse at 20 cents a night. Because Pierce found there was "no longer any opposition" in the legislature that year, it was not very exciting for him. Being one who thrived on conflict, he had to satisfy his yearning for excitement with competitive card games and fast sleigh rides.

At this time, Franklin and four others were selected to put up a slate of Jacksonian candidates for offices ranging from governor to congressional representative. A local newspaper said, "Franklin Pierce is the most popular man of his age in New Hampshire . . . he has a handsome person, bland and agreeable manners, a prompt and off-hand manner of saying and doing things, and talents competent to sustain himself in any station." Because of his popularity, Pierce was picked to be the congressional nominee on the ticket. And because the Jacksonian Democrats were very powerful in the state, he was easily elected.

Upon his election to Congress, Pierce wrote, "I am gratified tho' certainly not elated." He explained to friends that he was not as taken with the glamour of politics now that he knew more about its inner workings. He also felt guilty for neglecting his law profession, and still would rather have been a successful lawyer than a politician.

To the Nation's Capital

In the spring of 1833, Congressman-elect Pierce planned to take a trip around the United States before reporting to Washington. But there was an outbreak of cholera (a serious and contagious intestinal disease), so he had to change his plans.

Pierce decided instead to visit his sister Betsy and her husband in Boston. While there, he became seriously ill with a disease similar to cholera. Franklin was in terrible pain, and he lost a great deal of weight. He became so ill that he was near death. But after a time, he slowly began to regain his strength, and finally he recovered fully.

By November 21 Franklin was strong enough to travel to Washington. He set out from New Hampshire for the slow, tedious journey. After taking a stagecoach to Boston, he took another to a port on Long Island Sound. From there he sailed on a steamboat to New York City. He left New York on another boat and arrived in Perth Amboy, New Jersey. At Perth Amboy, he boarded a train that took him to Bordentown, New Jersey, where he took a steamboat down the Delaware River and docked in Philadelphia on the third night after leaving Boston. From Philadelphia, another boat took him to Newcastle, Delaware. Then there was another long train ride to Frenchtown, Delaware, a steamboat to Baltimore, Maryland, and, lastly, a stagecoach ride of 40 miles before Franklin reached the nation's capital. Needless to say, when he finally arrived in Washington on November 28, after a journey of seven days, he was tired, dirty, and happy to be there.

The New Fellow in Washington

Before long, New Hampshire's youngest congressman was living at Mrs. Hill's boardinghouse on Pennsylvania Avenue, near Third Street. Her four-story brick house was one of many congressional "messes" (the local name for boardinghouses) where senators and congressmen lived. Because their tenure in office was often short, the men did not want to build their own homes. Besides, most of their hometowns were too far away for their families to make the long journey to Washington very often. Congress usually met around the first of December, so the congressmen would arrive in late fall and stay until the session ended in March.

In Pierce's "mess" lived Senator and Mrs. Isaac Hill from New Hampshire, several other senators and congressmen, and some of their wives, mostly from other New England states. This group was soon joined by Benjamin French, another of Pierce's friends from back home, who was now an assistant to the clerk in the House of Representatives.

Mrs. Hill's mess was managed southern style. She had many black servants as well as dozens of slaves who acted as personal attendants to the guests. It was Franklin Pierce's first experience with slavery. Though the subject of slavery evoked much discussion among the New Hampshire delegation, Franklin did not seem to think much about it. He simply commented in a letter to a friend that there were slaves at Mrs. Hill's, but they were all properly married, neatly dressed, and they did a lot of singing.

At noon on December 2, 1833, Franklin Pierce was sworn in as a congressman, and he and the other 240 members began their work in the House of Representatives. The following week Pierce was appointed to the important Judiciary Committee. Every day he would travel wide, unpaved Pennsylvania Avenue in a horse-drawn coach that stopped at every corner to pick up passengers. On the coach, congressmen, foreign diplomats, and Cabinet officers rubbed elbows with clerks, tradesmen, and lobbyists.

CONGRESSMAN AT WORK

Pierce worked in the domed Capitol building, situated on a hill. Although the dome at that time was rather squat, the building was the crowning glory of the city. The Senate met in the north wing, and the Supreme Court, where Chief Justice John Marshall presided, sat in the basement. The Library of Congress was on the west front, and the House of Representatives in the south wing met in a heavily curtained semicircular room surrounded on all sides by enormous marble pillars. One of Pierce's friends remarked that you could feel the grandeur of the room "until you see the members."

Pierce's colleagues were an odd lot, some dirty, others hard-drinking, and many backwoods representatives so lacking in manners that they attended the sessions with their hats on. Yet Pierce was part of this diverse group, and with them he was soon working on the legislative problems of the nation.

Loyal to His Hero

In January 1834, President Jackson gave his State of the Union message (an annual speech by a President indicating the direction he hopes Congress will go in the coming year), and Pierce listened with enthusiasm. Because he agreed with the President that the United States should not have a national bank, Pierce voted against renewing the bank's charter when it expired in 1836. He also was definitely against supporting the bank with any government money until the charter ran out. Many opposed the President on this issue, but after much debate, the House voted its approval. Those who had been against the President formed the Whig coalition. For the time being, though, the Jacksonians still controlled Congress.

Franklin was scheduled to make his first speech in Congress, but because he became ill, the speech had to be postponed. Finally, on February 27, when he was feeling better, he spoke on the subject of pensions for Revolutionary War veterans. It was the highlight of the session for him.

Many Revolutionary War soldiers and their widows and orphans had made claims against the government. For years, each claim had been processed on an individual basis. But now Congress was debating a special bill that would cover all Revolutionary War payments.

Franklin spoke against the bill. He said that since the war had ended long ago, all the legitimate claims had already been settled. His speech earned much applause, and the bill was killed. Even John Quincy Adams, with whom Franklin almost always disagreed, approved of what Pierce had said.

The Daily Routine

After his speech, Franklin was busy with business that came before the Judiciary Committee. Besides his committee duties, there were claims by people and governments to be brought before various departments, petitions to be presented to Congress, and private bills to introduce and follow through committees. There were no private offices, secretaries, typewriters, or computers in those days. Pierce's work had to be done at his desk in the House of Representatives or in his room at Mrs. Hill's boardinghouse.

Franklin's daily routine was to get up early, breakfast at nine, and go to the House or to one of the government departments if he was doing business for some constituent (a person in his home district). He might attend a committee meeting or work at his desk until noon, when the House met in three- or four-hour sessions. Pierce would listen to the debates if they interested him, otherwise he would write letters or read newspapers, which was the custom of the majority of House members. There was no lunch break, but he could go to the basement of the House for a snack if he was hun-

gry. His big meal was dinner, served at Mrs. Hill's late in
the afternoon, and then he had a light supper after dark.

There were good times, too, for the high-spirited, young
congressman. He attended the President's reception on New
Year's Day and went to numerous parties. Pierce would also
go to the races, visit the theater, or take boat trips on a nearby
river or canal.

Standing on His Own

In 1834 Congressman Pierce voted against the Jacksonian
Democrats for the first time in his political career. He did
not approve of their wanting to give settlers on public lands
automatic rights to those lands. On the issue of internal improvements (roads, canals, harbors, etc.), although approved
by the President, he again voted against the administration.
Pierce's ideas went back to the Jeffersonian days, when it was
thought that the powers of the federal government should be
limited. He believed the states must be responsible for internal improvements and the granting of land rights.

When Franklin Pierce came home that summer, the people of his New Hampshire district nominated him to be their
congressman for a second term. Few men were sent back to
Washington a second time; Pierce was beginning to feel at
home in politics.

WEDDING BELLS RING

Now that Franklin was assured of a future in politics, he
decided to get married. Some time before, he had fallen in
love with Jane Means Appleton, the daughter of the late President Jesse Appleton of Bowdoin College. They had met often in her Amherst, Massachusetts, home, where they were
married on November 19, 1834, just before Franklin was to
return for the next session of Congress.

Jane, a shy, retiring woman who had tuberculosis, was

Pierce married Jane Means Appleton in 1834. Although she was a shy and retiring woman, she bravely tried to carry out her duties in the White House, when Pierce was President, despite ill health and the sorrow over the death of her three sons. (Library of Congress.)

quite different from Franklin. For one thing, she was the daughter of a well-established, extremely religious New England Federalist family, and she had strict ideas on how well-bred people should behave. Her husband, on the other hand, was a fun-loving, vain, hard-drinking, backwoods Democrat.

Shortly after their wedding, Pierce returned to Washington with his bride and settled in a boardinghouse for the winter. Slender and frail, Jane found the long journey very difficult. Benjamin French reported that Mrs. Pierce looked miserable when she arrived, but after a week or so, she was in much better health.

A Dull Session

During the next session of Congress, there was very little of importance for Franklin Pierce to do. He served on a committee that investigated the educational system of the United States Military Academy at West Point, New York. He was angered that many cadets would get a free education from the government and then resign their commissions after graduation. As a militiaman, Colonel Pierce disliked West Point. After the committee split in its recommendations, Pierce helped write the majority report against an appropriation bill for West Point. However, because the minority blocked the printing of the report, it did not come up before the House.

Although there was other business still pending, most congressmen wanted to leave, so the session ended on March 4. But because the rivers were still frozen, the northern congressmen could not go home. While Pierce remained in Washington, the congressional elections were held in New Hampshire and he was re-elected to a third term. But he did not hear about it until he returned to Hillsborough.

Pierce had bought a new home in Hillsborough, but Jane stayed with relatives in Lowell, Massachusetts, while he fixed it up. When she joined him in May, she found he had put in gravel walks, fences, and had even hung new wallpaper.

That summer, Albert Baker, a recent graduate of Dartmouth College, came to live with General Pierce and study law with Franklin. He kept the Pierce law office going while Franklin was away in Congress.

In the fall of 1835, when Pierce was ready to go back to Washington, Jane did not feel up to making the journey. Besides, she had found the capital dirty and rough, so she chose to spend the winter staying with relatives and friends. When Franklin joined the New Hampshire delegation in Washington, he missed his wife and wrote to her every day.

Chapter 4
Fighting and Feuding

Representative John Fairfield of Maine received a petition in December 1835 signed by 172 ladies of his state. It seemed to be nothing more than a bunch of church ladies praying for something unimportant. But it wasn't.

This petition happened to be the first attack on slave holding within the capital itself. It stated that slavery in the District of Columbia was "abominable" to all Americans who hated slavery. Because the District was federal property, Congress had the right to regulate slavery there and the moral obligation to wipe it out. The petition might not have attracted much attention among the dozens of petitions before Congress, but it came at a bad time. It was just two weeks after the slavery issue had begun to heat up in Washington, and it was like a firecracker being thrown into a fire.

FACING THE SLAVERY QUESTION

When Congress convened on December 1, 1835, Pierce's friend, James K. Polk of Tennessee, became Speaker of the House. Polk, a Jacksonian Democrat and a southern slaveholder who believed strongly in states' rights, appointed Pierce to several committees. But this session would mean more than just committee work to Pierce. Facing the political question of slavery for the first time, it would become the most important session in the many years he was a congressman.

Since 1820, the Missouri Compromise (the law making the southern boundary of Missouri the future dividing line between slave and free states in the Louisiana Purchase territory) had temporarily settled the slavery question. Because no new sates had applied for admittance recently, Congress had not been too concerned about slavery. But now the issue was being pressed by abolitionists, those who wanted to abolish slavery.

There were many reasons for revived interest in the slavery question. Britain had outlawed slave trade and was trying to suppress all such trade north of the Equator. Also, slavery had not become a part of the economics of the northern states as it had in the South. Thus, preachers, ladies and newspaper editors in the North could speak out against it freely. There was also the fact that storm clouds were gathering (although still in the distance) over the eventuality of Texas being admitted to the Union. Texas, about to break from Mexico, was a slave state. This helped the antislavery movement gain strength in the North.

States' Rights Versus the Federal Government

Pierce had been a believer in the doctrine of states' rights from early youth. Even when it came to important issues like slavery, he thought that the people of each state should decide the matter for themselves. He acknowledged that the Union was growing and changing, but he supported his position by saying that if the states had not agreed to limit the power of the federal government when preparing the Constitution, there would not have been a Union.

President Jackson, however, had undergone a change in his thinking about states' rights back in 1832, when he had to deal with South Carolina's refusal to obey the federal tax laws. He threatened to use force to make that state accept federal authority. The President then realized that for the Union to survive and grow, the doctrine of states' rights was not valid anymore. If Pierce had been a different type of person, he might have reconsidered his position on states' rights in light of President Jackson's changing attitude. However, once Pierce believed in something, he had a difficult time changing his mind.

That was how things stood in December 1835, when Congressman Fairfield presented the petition of the church ladies. From that time until the start of the Civil War in 1861, there was continuous debate in the United States about slavery. The southern states had become very touchy about the subject because abolitionists were flooding the South with propaganda. When the slaves heard that there were people up North who wanted them to be free, it was difficult for slaveholders to control them. As a result, Georgia passed a law in 1835 providing the death penalty to anyone who published material tending to incite slave rebellions.

Abolitionists Go Home!

That summer, the South became angrier and angrier. Abolitionist "agitators" were loaded into wagons and trains and shipped back North. Some were even tarred and feathered, others badly beaten. More determined than ever to end slavery, northern abolitionists retaliated by bombarding the South with written propaganda. To show their hatred for the abolitionist "meddlers," southerners burned a boatload of their materials in Charlestown harbor. The time had come for the issue to be fought out in Congress.

Pierce knew there were abolitionists in his home state, but he thought they were few in number. In a letter to Polk, he said, "I do not believe there is one person out of a hundred who does not wholly reprobate [condemn] the course of the few reckless fanatics who are able only to disturb occasionally the quiet of a village." And he made a speech in the House saying that New Hampshire people hated the abolitionists, using almost the same words that he had written to Polk.

Actually, there were many abolitionists in the Granite State; in Concord, they even had their own newspaper, the *Herald of Freedom.* That summer, one of the famous English abolitionists, George Thompson, spoke there and drew a large, cheering crowd. But a few rotten eggs were thrown, too, so there was some basis for Pierce's thinking that abolitionists were not very strong in New Hampshire.

Charged with Lying

In the Senate, John C. Calhoun of South Carolina attacked the northerners for their views on slavery. When New Hampshire Senator Isaac Hill countered with an attack on Calhoun and his supporters, Calhoun, angrily sent a copy of a clipping from the *Herald of Freedom* to the clerk's desk to be read aloud. The article quoted Congressman Pierce, saying that not one person in 500 in New Hampshire supported abolition. Then, as if to prove Pierce had deliberately lied, the Calhoun supporters circulated printed petitions that had been signed by New Hampshire people to show that there was indeed much sympathy for abolition in the Granite State.

Just as the clerk was reading the article aloud, Pierce came into the Senate. Hearing the charges against him, he quickly left the room. But the more he thought about it, the more determined he became to defend his good name. No one was going to call Franklin Pierce a liar!

Although Calhoun later apologized and said he meant no disrespect, Pierce answered his charges with a fiery speech on the House floor. The argument went on and on, becoming personal and emotional until Pierce became so angry that he challenged anyone to a duel who thought the article was true. Luckily, no one responded.

Calhoun's attack came at a time when Pierce was not well physically or emotionally. Their baby, Franklin, Jr., who had been born on February 2, 1836, had died three days later, and Jane was in extremely poor health. Pierce's unhappy frame of mind was possibly the reason he became involved in a scandalous episode. He was a sociable fellow who had a drinking problem—a weakness he believed he had inherited from his mother. One night, he had been drinking with two other congressmen before going to the theater. Upon their arrival at the theater, the three men found they were to share a box with an Army officer with whom one of the congressmen had quarreled earlier. The congressman drew a gun, and soon the theater was in an uproar. It became an unpleasant scandal, leaving Pierce very ill. He was never to forget the grief that February 1836 brought him.

Verbal Battlefield

When Pierce returned to Congress in March 1836, it was back to committee meetings, financial debates, and political maneuvers against the Whigs. Then in May, two serious issues came before the nation. One was the successful rebellion of Texas against Mexico and the fear of the abolitionists that Texas would be admitted to the Union as a slave state. Another more important one at that moment was the Pickney Committee report on abolitionist petitions in federal territories. After studying the question carefully, the committee had come to the conclusion that petitions urging Congress to end slavery, such as the one from the Maine ladies, should be accepted by Congress, then set aside and not acted upon.

Although setting aside the petitions did not solve the problem, in 1836 it seemed to be a good way to avoid handling a difficult issue. Pierce, with the majority of congressmen, voted for the Pickney resolution. He thought the country could be peaceful and prosperous if the little groups of hated abolitionist troublemakers were stopped.

But John Quincy Adams and other abolitionists protested vehemently against the "gag rule," as the Pickney resolution came to be known. Adams also led the fight against the annexation of Texas, declaring that the North would not allow another slave state in the Union. With all the bickering and yelling, the session became a nightmare.

When bills calling for Michigan and Arkansas to join the Union came up, there was a riot on the floor of the House, and fights broke out in the press gallery. After five days of disorderly debate, concluding with a 25-hour session of constant shouting, the bills passed. In the midst of all this feuding, Pierce was selected to be Speaker *pro tem* of the House to chair the stormy session in Polk's absence.

When the month of June arrived, the congressmen were anxious to go home, but they had to stay in Washington because of unfinished business. Pierce again spoke against appropriations to educate West Point men who had no intention of staying in the Army after their graduation. But the appropriations bill passed anyway, and the session finally came to a close.

The country had been in a depression for a few years. That summer when Pierce went over his finances, he found they were in poor shape. He put his house up for sale but there were no buyers, so he had to borrow $500 to pay his bills before returning to Washington.

SENATOR PIERCE

When Senator Isaac Hill was elected governor of New Hampshire in 1836, Pierce's friends wanted to nominate him for Hill's Senate seat when the state legislature met later in the fall. In the meantime, Representative Pierce, accompanied by his wife, went back to work in Washington. Jane was almost never well and did not go out much, but sociable Pierce made some new friends, including Jefferson Davis of Mississippi.

The Pierces had barely settled in their new boarding-house when they received word that the New Hampshire legis-lature had elected the 34-year-old Pierce senator for a full six-year term. But before moving to the other side of the Cap-itol building, the new senator had to finish his duties as a representative. He still served on the Judiciary Committee and several others. Once again he took part in angry discus-sions about slavery petitions, and during the confusing, hec-tic last week of the session, the congressmen tried to cram everything in so they could finish all business by March 4, 1837.

But as soon as that session was over, the next one be-gan, and Pierce moved to the Senate to attend the inaugura-tion of Martin Van Buren as eighth President of the United States. After Van Buren's Cabinet appointments were ap-proved, the Pierces were finally able to go home.

The Panic of 1837

When the depression began, Pierce blamed the Bank of the United States. It had kept money so tight that when its char-ter expired in 1836, local bankers loosened credit restrictions drastically. Now the country's banking system was in a state of chaos and people had lost confidence in all banks.

In September 1837, President Van Buren called a spe-cial session of Congress to deal with these financial prob-lems. The President asked for a new, sound currency backed by gold and silver. He proposed issuing $10 million in notes or bonds to cover the government's debts. He also proposed that importers pay their customs fees with paper money in-stead of gold. And he outlined a new system where there would be subtreasuries in various parts of the country so the government could control its own money. Senator Pierce voted for the bills, and most of the President's proposals passed.

Because of the special session, Pierce did not make money as a lawyer that year, but he was pleased that Albert Baker had passed the bar and could now handle his law business while he was away. In December, when the Pierces left for Washington, Senator Pierce's law firm was in Baker's capable hands.

The Youngest Senator

Coming from the crowded House of Representatives, the Senate chamber seemed luxurious to Senator Pierce. At his large desk, he felt quite important in this dignified and powerful body of 52 men, which included Henry Clay of Kentucky, John C. Calhoun of South Carolina, and Daniel Webster of Massachusetts. These three famous men were called the "Great Triumvirate," and their opinions pretty much controlled Congress from 1825 to 1850. Although he was a fine orator, Pierce's speeches seldom attracted much public attention. As in the House, Pierce was assigned to several committees, but there were no indications of his being an innovative leader.

Hot Tempers

Because Texas was a slave state, many northerners wanted to refuse its admission to the Union. Senator Calhoun, determined to protect the rights of slave states, entered several resolutions to that effect, and Franklin Pierce voted for them. Pierce explained that three years earlier he had thought the South was too touchy about the subject of slavery, but now he feared that a few abolitionist fanatics and scheming politicians would cause the end of the Democratic Party and eventually the Union. Again, it was a matter of principle with Pierce—the principle of states' rights. He despised the Whigs of New England because he felt they had used the issue of slavery and abolitionists for their own purposes without thinking about principle.

Henry Clay: The Great Pacificator

Henry Clay was a leading American statesman for 40 years. He was born on April 12,
1777, in Hanover County, Virginia, had very
little formal schooling, and by age 14 was
working in a store. But young Clay had a
sharp mind and liked to read, so he decided
to become a lawyer. He was admitted to the
Virginia bar in 1797 and soon had a successful practice in Lexington, Kentucky. Locally,
he was well known for his oratory, but it was
his criminal cases that made him famous
throughout the nation. He is credited with
being the first to use the plea of ''temporary
insanity'' to save an accused man from the
death sentence.

Clay's political career began in 1801
when he was made a member of the Kentucky Constitutional Convention. In 1803 he
was elected to the Kentucky legislature, and
he then served two unexpired terms in the
United States Senate from 1806 to 1807 and
again from 1809 to 1811. But he preferred to
serve in the less-dignified House of Representatives. He entered the House in 1811 and
was elected Speaker on the first day of the
session. Five more times he was re-elected to
the House and the Speakership, and he held
the office until 1825 with the exception of
the 1821–1823 term, when he returned to
his law practice.

Clay argued strongly for the War of 1812
and was made a peace commissioner at the
end of the war. He was one of the signers of

the Treaty of Ghent in 1814. After the war, Clay became an ardent nationalist. He favored a national bank, protective tariffs, and government support of internal improvements. He called it his "American System," designed to promote friendship in all sections of the country. His strong views made him a leader of the National Republican Party, later called the Whigs.

Clay often said the purpose of his public life was to preserve the Union. He tried to settle disputes between proslavery and anti-slavery groups and believed compromise was the best way to peace. In 1820 Clay used his influence to get the Missouri Compromise passed, and it brought him the informal title "The Great Pacificator." He also helped arrange the Compromise Tariff of 1833, when South Carolina threatened to withdraw from the Union. Clay made his last great speech in the Senate in support of the Compromise of 1850, which postponed civil war for 10 years.

With John Calhoun and Daniel Webster, Clay was part of the "Great Triumvirate" of senators. Of the three, Clay, a generous, charming and witty man, was the most popular. But despite his popularity, Clay never achieved the one thing he wanted most—to become President of the United States. He ran for the office three times, but was always defeated. As secretary of state under John Quincy Adams, Clay worked for friendly relations with Latin American countries.

In 1839 Clay gave a speech stating he was against slavery, but he blamed the abolitionists for the disputes that were threatening to break up the Union. When Clay's friends told him that his speech would ruin his chances of being President, he made his famous remark, "I'd rather be right than President."

Henry Clay was 75 years old when he died in 1852, the year Franklin Pierce was elected President.

During 1838, Pierce became involved in an incident that showed just how hot the political tempers of the time were. Jonathan Cilley, a Democrat from Maine, was Pierce's close friend. Together, they consistently provoked the Whigs in speeches on the Senate floor. Their actions finally led to a duel in which Cilley was killed. Pierce was shaken; he had not only lost a friend, but the newspapers were blaming him for arranging the affair. He wrote a letter explaining that he had tried to stop the duel, but the Whigs still blamed him, making Pierce hate them even more. Pierce eventually came to believe that the Whigs had planned the murder of his friend Cilley.

RETIRING FROM POLITICS

Pierce's term in the Senate was not up until 1843, but he was disillusioned with politics because of Cilley's death and the slavery issue. Because he did not expect to be re-elected anyway, he began to think about leaving the political scene early. Jane was delighted. She hated Washington and had said many times, "Oh how I wish he was out of political life." Although

Mr. and Mrs. Pierce had lived in boardinghouses most of their married life. This Concord, New Hampshire, residence was their first real home. It was sold during the Mexican-American War. (Library of Congress.)

it was to take him four years to make up his mind, Pierce began to plan for his political retirement by forming a law partnership with Asa Fowler in Concord.

Pierce hoped to make more money in the New Hampshire capital. His Senate pay had barely covered personal expenses, and he had no savings. The Pierces moved to Concord in August 1838, leaving Albert Baker to run the Hillsborough law practice and to look after ailing General Pierce and his wife. Home ties were broken when Pierce's mother died that year, followed by his father's death in 1839 at the age of 81.

In September 1839 a son, Frank Robert, was born. When Pierce went back to Washington, Jane stayed home with the new baby. Congress had many important matters to consider, including having to face Britain's anger because of American sympathy for a Canadian rebellion. On the domestic front, Senator Pierce still stood firm for states' rights. If certain states wanted a railroad, let them supply the money. Improvements to rivers and harbors? Fine! Let the states do their own and not ask the people of New Hampshire to pay for something that Maine wanted. As for Texas, Pierce voted with the majority, putting the matter of annexation on hold.

During the 1838 and 1839 congressional sessions, Pierce mostly handled routine bills pertaining to veteran's pensions. In 1840, politics became more exciting. The Whig Party had gained strength and fought the Democrats by choosing William Henry Harrison to run as its candidate for President. Pierce thought Van Buren was the better man, and although they were no longer friends, Pierce, always the good Democrat, campaigned for him. Although Van Buren carried New Hampshire by 6,000 votes, he was defeated nationally by Harrison.

With the hated Whigs now in control, Pierce spent his last two sessions in Congress as a minority party member. When Harrison caught a cold in the inaugural parade and died a few weeks later, Vice-President John Tyler became President. Pierce continued to battle Clay and Webster in the Senate, but his heart was not in it.

On February 16, 1842, Pierce finally retired to Concord amid warm wishes for happiness from friends and opponents alike. The old general would have been proud of the praise his senator son received.

Chapter 5
Marching to War

W hen Franklin Pierce retired from the U.S. Senate in 1842, he assumed he was retiring from politics. But the Democratic Party in New Hampshire was in a sorry state, and his political know-how was desperately needed. Jane had hoped he was finished with politics forever, but few politicians leave the political arena at the young age of 38. Besides, Pierce's friends would not let him quit. They made him chairman of the State Central Committee of the Democratic Party, and he became a party "boss."

GRANITE STATE "BOSS"

Just a few hours after his arrival in Concord, Pierce made a speech at the courthouse. In addition to talking about the issues of Texas and slavery, a new issue – the railroad – had surfaced. New Hampshire farmers were against railroads because they thought their farmland might be overrun by the railroad builders. After joining the antirailroad group, Pierce then spent two weeks speaking against the Whigs throughout the state – in a different town every night.

No longer under the influence of his father or party elders, Franklin Pierce demonstrated that he was able to think and act independently. When he gave up drinking and became the chairman of the state temperance society, Jane was very proud. The Pierces were quite happy. Concord was an exciting town, and after living in boardinghouses most of their married life, they were in their first real home. Another son, Benjamin, had been born on April 13, 1841, and with their two young sons, they dreamed of a wonderful future. All went well for the Pierces until November 14, 1843, when their four-year-old son Frank died of typhus fever. His death was a severe blow to the family.

A year later, the Democrats nominated James Polk as their candidate for President. Pierce was delighted because he and Polk were on the same side of many questions. Polk was a moderate on the slavery issue and was trying to accomplish a diplomatic and political miracle by bringing about a compromise. Pierce did not see how it could be done, but he was for Polk all the way.

A Split in the Ranks

Once again, Pierce was chosen to be chairman of the Democratic Party in New Hampshire. He promised candidate Polk that the Democrats would carry the state by 6,000 to 10,000 votes. Pierce stumped the campaign trail until he was exhausted. True to Pierce's word, Polk carried New Hampshire by almost 10,000 votes! Polk was so appreciative that in 1845 he appointed Pierce federal district attorney for New Hampshire.

At this time, New Hampshiremen were deciding what to do about slavery in Texas. Most of the people in the Granite State did not want to admit another slave state into the Union. Pierce attended many town meetings where he and his friends emphasized that if the United States did not admit Texas, Great Britain would. And if that happened, it would give the hated British a foothold on American soil.

But now there was a rift in the Democratic Party because New Hampshire Congressman John P. Hale would not support the annexation of Texas. Pierce wielded so much power in the state that he and his friends (the statehouse ring) kept Hale from being re-elected.

But Hale did not stay defeated. He became a Free-Soil Democrat, allied himself with the Whigs, and organized an antistatehouse ring. Pierce warned the Democrats many times of the danger of "this unpatriotic alliance." When Pierce's law partner, Asa Fowler, sided with Hale, Pierce broke up the firm and formed a new partnership with Josiah Minot, another talented lawyer. Hale's alliance with the Whigs proved to be good for him; in 1846 the Whigs sent him to the United States Senate. Hale never forgot that Franklin Pierce was his enemy.

WAR WITH MEXICO

When newspapers brought word that American soldiers had been killed on U.S. soil by Mexican invaders, President Polk declared war on Mexico in May 1846. In New Hampshire, the people called it a slaveholders' war, and many men refused to fight. Franklin Pierce, the loyal Democrat who had always dreamed of a military career, volunteered as a private, but he was not called up to serve.

Instead, President Polk offered Pierce the Cabinet post of attorney general. Pierce may have been tempted to return to Washington, but he refused the position in order to stay at home with his family. He also said that he would decline any public office "except at the call of my country in time of war." When, on February 15, 1847, a bill was passed to increase the size of the army, Pierce was appointed a colonel for the duration of the war. Soon after, he was made a brigadier general.

Pierce's chance for honor and glory in the field of battle had arrived. But first, he had to buy equipment and recruit the men for his brigade. When this was done, a fine, black horse was provided by his political friends, and he left Con-

The Mexican-American War

When Texas declared its independence from the Mexican government in 1836, Mexico warned the United States that, if Texas joined the Union, it would declare war. All was quiet for eight years until James Polk was elected President and said he wanted to admit Texas to the Union. The very next year, in December 1845, Texas became a state, and Mexico broke off relations with the United States.

But Mexico stopped short of declaring war, and the two countries could have settled their differences at the bargaining table except that other disputes came up, too. One was the question of the boundary between Texas and Mexico. Texas claimed the Rio Grande River as its southern border. Mexico said the boundary was the Nueces River. There was also the dispute over $3 million Mexico owed the United States—compensation for American lives and property lost during Mexico's many revolutions. Another problem concerned American settlers who were moving steadily westward into Mexican territory and were quarreling with the Mexicans.

President Polk appointed former Congressman John Slidell of Louisiana minister to Mexico. He instructed Slidell to tell Mexico that the United States would cancel all claims against it if Mexico would accept the Rio Grande boundary and sell New Mexico and California to the United States for $25 million. If Mexico refused to sell New Mexico and California, Slidell was to offer to cancel the claims on condition that Mexico agree to the Rio Grande boundary.

When Slidell arrived in Mexico, another revolution was going on and there were now two presidents. Both presidents refused to see Slidell because they were afraid of being called cowards if they made deals with the United States. Slidell then reported to Polk that Mexico needed to be taught a lesson.

In the meantime, Polk had ordered General Zachary Taylor, who was stationed at the Nueces River with 3,000 men, to advance to the Rio Grande. Then a small army of American cavalrymen was met by a larger army of Mexicans on April 15 and was defeated in battle. Polk had already decided to ask Congress to declare war on Mexico, and this skirmish gave him the excuse to say, "Mexico had invaded our territory and shed American blood on American soil." Mexico, however, had as good a claim as the United States to the soil where the blood was shed. But on May 13, 1846, Congress declared war on Mexico.

As a result of the war, the United States gained more than 525,000 square miles of territory, which became the states of California, Nevada, Utah, most of Arizona and New Mexico, and parts of Colorado and Wyoming. But the war also renewed the bitter quarrels over slavery in the United States. The big question was: Should the conquered territory be slave or free? The Mexican-American War was one of many factors leading to the Civil War.

cord amid the cheers of a large crowd. Pierce felt he was fulfilling his patriotic duty by going to war. His only regret was in leaving his dear wife and son Benjamin.

Off to Veracruz

When Pierce's friend, Nathaniel Hawthorne, came to Boston to see Pierce off, Hawthorne commented, "General Pierce seemed to be in his element, looking fit and in good spirits." On May 27, Pierce's brigade sailed for Veracruz, Mexico, to join General Zachary Taylor's army.

After war had been declared, the U.S. Army had moved into Mexico and won several victories, but now the fighting was at a standstill. General Winfield Scott had taken Veracruz that spring and then stopped at Puebla to reorganize his troops. On June 27, General Pierce and his detachment of 2,500 men arrived at Veracruz. His orders were to form a wagon train, join Scott's army at Puebla, and march together toward Mexico City.

Veracruz was a hot, muggy swampland where illness was rampant, so Pierce ordered his men to Vergara, where they pitched their tents on a sandy beach. Although they were ordered to join Scott's army as quickly as possible, no transportation was available for the long march. They had collected 2,000 wild mules, but then the mules had stampeded and most of them had run away. General Pierce and his brigade had to wait until more wild mules were rounded up and trained to wear a harness and bridle.

The Long March to Puebla

On July 12, 1847, a shipload of 80 horses arrived from New Orleans, and at last Pierce's army could prepare to advance. Supplies were loaded into wagons, horses and mules were hitched up, and two days later, the first section of the wagon train moved out. Pierce, along with the rest of the men and

When the war with Mexico was declared, Pierce volunteered and was made a colonel; later he was promoted to the rank of brigadier general. He embarked for Mexico with his troops in May 1847, took part in several battles, and returned home in December of the same year. (Library of Congress.)

40 wagons, did not leave until late afternoon of the third day. The going was slow and difficult. Wagons sank in mud over their wheels, mules were unmanageable, and the men were sick from disease and the terrible heat. Five torturous hours later, the brigade had advanced only three miles.

The next morning, Pierce got the wagon train on the road by four o'clock. Rumbling over short, steep hills, they slowly advanced five more miles. The wagon train kept on through drenching rain and extreme heat, up hills and through swamps, making just a few miles at a time until they reached a highway paved with cement that stretched from the coast to Mexico City. The cement highway made it much easier for the wagon train to advance. But because of the extreme heat, the brigade only marched in early morning and late afternoon, constantly on the alert for enemy attack.

Then, on July 19, Pierce's brigade was fired on by snipers, but American guns quickly drove off the small enemy band. About a mile farther on, the Mexicans struck again, and Pierce's men returned the fire. But this time, before the enemy was driven off, several Mexicans were killed and a number of American soldiers were wounded.

A Surprise Assault

The march continued, and two days later the brigade came to National Bridge (one of the many bridges that spanned streams crossed by the highway). Scouts reported that the enemy was camped in a village beyond the bridge. General Pierce surveyed the situation from the top of a hill. Down below was the Antigua River, spanned by the bridge. Beyond it, on top of a little rise, was the village with a breastwork (a hastily constructed fortification) that looked down on the bridge. Most of the Mexicans were behind the breastwork. There was no way to cross the bridge without being blasted by the enemy. But how were they to reach the Mexicans if they did not cross the bridge? General Pierce planned a surprise assault.

With cannons booming behind them, Pierce's troops charged across the bridge and up the hill into the breastwork. The breastwork was beyond the range of Pierce's guns, but the Mexicans did not know it. The thundering guns, together with the charge of the Americans, scared the untrained Mexican troops. As Pierce's men began to climb the barricade, the Mexicans broke and ran. They had fought bravely for a few minutes, wounding five Americans and sending a ball through General Pierce's hat. But soon the American flag flew above the village.

A few days later, the brigade made camp at the outskirts of Jalapa. After requisitioning supplies and paying what they thought was a fair price for them, they headed for La Hoya, a dangerous mountain pass. They went through the pass unharmed, and on August 6 finally reached Puebla. General Pierce had brought the long wagon train and 2,500 men safely through 150 miles of enemy territory in three weeks. Although they had been attacked many times and disease had been rampant, they had arrived at their destination with very few casualties. But there was little time for self-congratulation, because General Scott was eager to begin marching on the capital. He ordered some of his divisions to leave immediately, and on August 10, General Gideon Pillow's division, which included Pierce's brigade, moved out with the cry, "On to Mexico City!"

FOR HONOR AND GLORY

When the army of 11,000 reached a point about 20 miles from Mexico City, Pierce's brigade was ordered to move forward near San Augustin to fight the army of General Valencia. They were about 20 miles from their target on August 18, 1847, and the plan was for Pierce's men, along with another brigade, to charge from the front while a flank movement went on simultaneously.

When the cry of "Attack!" came, General Pierce mounted his black horse and, from atop a little hill, urged his men on. Then he led them into a field of heavy artillery fire. Shells exploded in every direction, making Pierce's horse jump. The general fell forward in the saddle and was struck in the groin by the saddle horn. The horse stumbled, went down, and the general was knocked unconscious. An aide shouted to Colonel Truman Ransom, second in command, to take charge of the brigade. Because Ransom could not hear the aide, an officer named George Morgan yelled, "Take command of the brigade, General Pierce is a . . . coward."

But a few minutes later, Pierce regained consciousness and saw to his regret that his fine steed had broken its leg. Slowly, the general got to his feet and tried to walk. But besides his groin injury, his left knee was severely wrenched, and he could barely hobble. As soon as Pierce received first aid, he found another horse, had an aide lift him into the saddle, and insisted on rejoining his brigade.

That night, Pierce was the senior officer in the field. It was raining, so he withdrew his force to a sheltered area. Later, with very little sleep, and feeling ill and worn, Pierce rejoined the brigade in an attack toward the rear of General Santa Anna's army. When General Scott saw Pierce astride his horse with one foot in the stirrup and one hanging limp, he told him to go back to the base. "For God's sake, General," Pierce protested, "this is the last great battle, and I must lead my brigade."

Intent on gaining honor and glory, Pierce led his men forward. Then, while creeping through a wide ditch under fire, he twisted his injured knee and again fainted from the pain. As an aide was carrying him from the field, Pierce came to and ordered him to stop. He had been called a coward before, and he would rather die than let that happen again. So he lay on the ground, in severe pain, peppered by Mexican bullets for hours during the Battle of Churubusco.

Without Pierce to lead them, his men failed to win their objective. But the war was won on another battlefield, and Santa Anna asked for a truce. To avoid more killing, General Scott agreed. So instead of marching into Mexico City as a conqueror, Pierce and two other brigadier generals were appointed to arrange the terms of the truce.

The War Goes On and On

But the truce negotiations failed. American soldiers then wanted to march into Mexico City, and they blamed Pierce, who was backing the truce, for cheating them out of the spoils of war. Pierce was hearing the word "coward" again. Some time before, George Morgan, the soldier who had called Pierce a coward on the battlefield, had learned the truth of what had happened and retracted his thoughtless words. But the damage to Pierce's reputation had been done.

Early in September, the fighting began again. General Worth was dispatched to capture the fortress of Molina del Rey, which Santa Anna was supposedly using for a cannon-ball factory. Pierce, who had been in reserve, was sent in later to help. He arrived near the end of the fighting and did nothing heroic. After that came the Battle of Chapultepec, and, as luck would have it, General Pierce was in bed with a severe case of dysentery while the battle raged. To his sorrow, his friend, Colonel Ransom, was killed commanding the troops.

As the battle continued, Pierce could not bear the thought of his men entering Mexico City without him. Sick as he was, he got out of bed, dressed, and rode his horse to the front. He arrived as the final assault was about to begin. Just as General Pierce prepared to lead his troops into battle—his one last chance for glory—a white flag of surrender was flown by the Mexicans, and the U.S. Army marched into the city without firing a single shot. Three months of garrison duty followed the surrender. Pierce planned to go home as soon as peace was assured, but the Mexican government was in chaos, and peace negotiations dragged on.

Home at Last

Finally, Pierce received his orders, and on December 8, General Scott gave a farewell dinner for him and another general who was leaving. Pierce had been well liked in the Army. He was especially close to several fellow officers with whom he formed a club. These men were to play a significant part in his life later on.

Arriving in the United States on December 28, 1847, Pierce reported first to President Polk in Washington and then took a leave of absence. He went to Lowell, where Jane was staying, and had a joyful reunion with his family. When he returned home, the people of Concord welcomed their war hero with cheers and church bells.

Early the following year, a peace treaty was finally signed and the war was officially over. Pierce went to Washington in February and resigned his commission. He had served his country in time of need, and although he had not gained much glory on the battlefield, he had done his duty. Now he wanted to be done with public life forever.

Chapter 6

"He's a Dictator!"

After the Mexican-American War, Franklin Pierce was a powerful force in keeping the Democratic Party in New Hampshire together despite its difficulties with slavery-related problems. Never changing his views on states' rights, he was often heard saying with a great deal of emotion that the rights of South Carolina or some other southern state must be protected as well as the rights of New Hampshire.

"He's a dictator!" some said of Pierce, because to them he was a powerful, ruthless Democrat and a slave sympathizer. But his friends called him the "Grand Man" and wanted him to run for President.

THE GOOD LIFE

For Franklin and Jane Pierce, the four years after the Mexican-American War were good years. Pierce was a respected member of the community, a popular party leader, and he was finally making money in his law practice. Because their home in Concord had been sold during the war, they made arrangements to live with Mr. and Mrs. Willard Williams on South Main Street in Concord. And after the loss of two young sons, the Pierces were happy to see Benjamin approaching his tenth birthday and growing up healthy. Now that Jane was away from Washington, she was feeling better than she had in a long time.

Franklin Pierce was considered to be one of the foremost trial lawyers in the state. He had a special talent to sway juries. A master of words, he would orchestrate his voice the way a violinist does his music to convince jury members to be on his side. Pierce handled civil and criminal cases. These included murder, libel, forgery, damage suits, and a new classification, corporation law, which meant representing banks, railroads, and mill owners.

Trouble Among the Democrats

Although the private life of Franklin Pierce was going very well, it was a different story for the Democratic Party. Except for the term of President John Quincy Adams, "the hated Federalist," the Democrats had occupied the presidency since 1800. But after almost 50 years in power, the slavery issue was beginning to break up the party.

Pierce had been offered the Democratic nomination to run for governor of New Hampshire, but he refused, saying that his only interest was in local politics, not in holding an office. He did not even attend the 1848 Democratic National Convention in Baltimore because he was busy with his law work and felt removed from national politics.

Because Polk refused to run for a second term, the Democrats slated Lewis Cass of Michigan as their candidate for President and General William Butler of Kentucky for Vice-President.

The Whigs, who were gaining strength, nominated General Zachary Taylor, the hero of the Mexican-American War, to run for President and Millard Fillmore of New York for Vice-President. Americans were looking for a wise man to solve the problem of slavery in Texas and the territories. They knew Taylor was a Louisiana slaveholder, but he had been brave and strong in battle, and he was devoted to the

Union. Taylor was elected and tried his best to be the wise leader that everyone wanted. But with Congress divided, and the Free-Soilers (who were against extending slavery) in the majority, it was practically impossible.

THE COMPROMISE OF 1850

After Taylor's election, Congress and the nation were involved in bitter political strife over whether the territory won from Mexico as a result of the war should have slavery or not. Finally Henry Clay, "The Great Pacificator," introduced in Congress a number of bills, called the Compromise of 1850, that were designed to settle the matter.

To please the South, the compromise gave Texas $10 million for its claims to New Mexican territory, promised no interference with slavery already existing in the District of Columbia, and set up a stricter federal law for the return of runaway slaves, called the Fugitive Slave Law. For the North, slave trade was abolished in the District of Columbia, and California was to come into the Union as a free state. The territories of New Mexico (including what is now Arizona) and Utah were organized, and the question of slavery was left to each of them to decide.

Congress passed the laws, and for a few years it seemed as if the Compromise of 1850 had solved the slavery problem. But abolitionists hated the Fugitive Slave Law, which they said they would not obey because Congress had no right to interfere with the states. Through a secret network called the underground railroad, many people helped thousands of escaped slaves travel north from one "station" to another. Southerners were angry that abolitionists helped slaves escape, usually to Canada, rather than send them back to their owners.

Strong Man in State Politics

The Fugitive Slave Law became an important issue in the politics of New Hampshire. The Democrats were not pleased with the election of Zachary Taylor, but when Taylor died after only 16 months in office, there was new hope for a Democratic victory in the 1852 presidential election. Rallying around Levi Woodbury, an old friend of Pierce's and a longtime Democrat, for President, New Hampshire Democrats pulled the state party together. That fall, Franklin Pierce toured the state on behalf of the Compromise of 1850, trying to convince people that, although New Hampshire was a northern state, it could live with the Fugitive Slave Law and still maintain the Union.

Pierce also served as chairman of the New Hampshire Constitutional Convention in 1850. For two months, the delegates worked to revise the old state constitution, which contained a provision barring Catholics from holding office. Since 1844 Pierce had been advocating that this be changed. But the voters rejected the work of the convention, and the delegates met again and tried to salvage some of the amendments. To Pierce's disappointment, at election time the amendment that would have given Catholics office-holding privileges was again defeated.

While this was going on, a number of Free-Soil Democrats had maneuvered the nomination of Reverend John Atwood as the Democratic candidate for governor of New Hampshire. Pierce approved of Atwood's nomination until he found that Atwood had rejected the validity of the Compromise of 1850, and particularly the Fugitive Slave Law. So, using his political influence, Pierce convinced the State Democratic Committee to select another candidate. They did so, and the Democrats replaced Atwood with Governor Samuel Dinsmoor, Jr., who was subsequently re-elected. Atwood's friends protested vigorously, calling Pierce and his "Concord

Clique" dictators. But Pierce responded with charges of party disloyalty. The Atwood affair demonstrated Pierce's power in New Hampshire and the strength of his belief in the preservation of the Union. He was 46 years old, had no ambition to hold office, and wanted only to keep a strong hand in local politics.

THE UNDECLARED CANDIDATE

Nobody from New England had been elected President after John Quincy Adams was defeated in 1824 for a second term in office. The South was against New Englanders because of the abolitionists' influence there, yet both Whigs and Democrats were searching for a man whose personal popularity could rise above the slavery issue. Sometimes people voted for a man they trusted instead of considering party platforms and issues.

But there was no escaping the slavery question. Sooner or later, people would realize that because of the geography of the United States, the balance of power among the states was not going to work out evenly. If the western lands had been cotton and tobacco country, like the slave section of the nation, it might have been possible to keep the balance of power evenly divided. But the West was not slave country, and California's antislavery constitution meant the end of hope for slavery in the Far West, too.

Democrats in Confusion

In September 1851, Levi Woodbury died. He had been the New England Democrats' leading hope for the presidential nomination, and his death left the party in a state of confusion. The Democrats searched frantically for a new man — a compromise candidate who could win the election. It could not be Lewis Cass because he had already been defeated once. Senator Hannibal Hamlin of Massachusetts was suggested, but he was not well known nationally. Many thought that General William Butler of Kentucky, who had run with Cass in 1848, might have a good chance. Other possibilities were James Buchanan of Pennsylvania, Stephen Douglas of Illinois, and William Marcy of New York.

Franklin Pierce was busy trying corporate law cases when he heard that Reverend Atwood, who was again running for state office, was calling him a dictator and a slave sympathizer. Pierce made several speeches defending his position. He said he was not a "boss," and he disliked slavery and the Fugitive Slave Law. But slavery was recognized in the Constitution. It was one of the compromises that had been accepted to make possible its adoption. Because he believed in the Constitution and loved the Union, he was willing to accept what he disliked to prevent lawmakers from breaking up the nation.

Pierce's powerful arguments appealed to many who had not previously understood why it seemed that he sympathized with the South. State Democrats began talking about Pierce's return to national politics.

Support for Pierce

In March 1852, General Butler, the leading contender for the Democratic presidential nomination, dropped out of the race. A group of Mexican-American War generals, led by Caleb Cushing and Gideon Pillow, then got together to control the nomination of the Democratic Party. They came up with the name of Franklin Pierce. When Cushing and Pillow met in Washington, they found there was already a quiet rally of support for Pierce going on there, too, but Pierce supporters did not know if he would accept the nomination.

It was at this time when Pierce's friend, Benjamin French, wrote the letter inviting Franklin to be the Democratic candidate for the 1852 presidential election. In January, when Pierce had been named New Hampshire's favorite son, he did not think he had a chance at the nomination. Now it was April, and he answered French that he would leave it to his friends in Washington to determine what his duty was. Then Pierce received a similar letter from Edmund Burke, another New Hampshire politician, urging him to enter the contest.

While General Pillow and Cushing were rounding up support for Pierce, they stopped in Concord to tell him his chances were excellent. Pierce welcomed the generals, but he insisted that his name not be used unless the convention became deadlocked and the delegates could not agree on one of the declared candidates.

Now it was no longer a secret that Pierce was a possible candidate. In May the editor of a Richmond, Virginia, newspaper asked Pierce to answer three questions about the Compromise of 1850 that he was asking each of the presidential candidates. But Pierce did not want to answer because he was not yet a declared candidate. Nevertheless, his political allies advised him to put his views in writing, so he wrote a letter to a friend outlining his basic political position. In it he said that the Compromise of 1850 measures should be "firmly maintained or the plain rights secured by the Constitution would be trampled in the dust." Again he stated that it did not make any difference if the outrage fell on South Carolina or New Hampshire – everyone's rights were important, and he would never endanger the Union. He ended by saying:

> If we of the North, who stood by the constitutional rights of the South, are to be abandoned to any time-serving policy, the hopes of democracy and the Union must sink together. As I told you, my name will not be before the convention, but I cannot help feeling that what there is to be done will be important beyond men and parties – transcendently important to the hopes of democratic progress and civil liberty.

A Surprise Nomination

When the Democratic Convention met in Baltimore on June 1, 1852, Pierce's name was not mentioned openly. It appeared that Cass would be the presidential candidate until the 49th ballot, when Franklin Pierce won the Democratic nomination. The surprise caused Mrs. Pierce to faint and become sullen and moody for days. Telegrams congratulating her husband poured in, and Pierce tried to take her away from all the excitement. But it followed them wherever they went.

The peace and quiet Jane needed had again been broken by politics. Pierce rationalized that he was willing to take on the demanding duties of the presidency for his son, so he would have a more satisfying life. But Benjamin wrote his mother that he hoped his father would not be elected. He did not want to live in Washington, and he knew she felt the same way.

A committee came to Concord to officially notify Pierce of his nomination, with William R. King of Alabama as the vice-presidential candidate. Pierce's Whig opponent would be his old commander in the Mexican-American War, General Winfield Scott.

A "Front Porch Campaign"

Pierce conducted a "front porch campaign." He answered letters and received visitors at home, but it was the party leaders who traveled the country for him. Pierce's position on slavery still confused many people. He called the Fugitive Slave Law morally wrong, but he demanded that it be enforced. When questioned further, Pierce said he had been misrepresented. He let the North and the South puzzle over which part was misrepresented. Pierce's old friend, Nathaniel Hawthorne, wrote a flattering campaign biography to help him get elected.

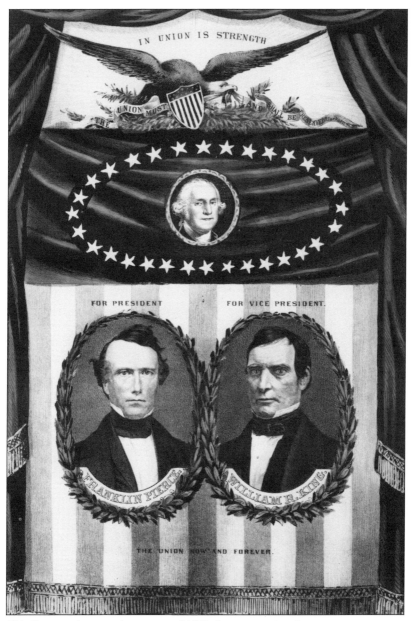

This Democratic campaign poster of 1852 shows portraits of Pierce for President, and William R. King of Alabama for Vice-President. For their presidential candidate, the Whigs nominated General Winfield Scott, who had gained fame in the Mexican-American War. (Library of Congress.)

Both major candidates had to endure a lot of humiliation and name calling. Charges of drunkenness and cowardice surfaced to plague Pierce again, and an old court-martial of Scott's was brought up. The candidates seemingly ignored these accusations, but when Pierce was called anti-Catholic because of New Hampshire's constitutional provision, he denied it vehemently and was provoked into making speeches.

On election day of 1852, results trickled in slowly. But by eleven o'clock that night, Pierce knew he was the President-elect of the United States. He had carried 27 states with 1,601,274 votes, and Scott had captured only four—Tennessee, Massachusetts, Kentucky, and Vermont—with 1,386,580 votes.

Chapter 7

Success and Tragedy

Success turned into tragedy for the Pierces early in 1853. On January 6, they boarded the train for Concord in Boston with their son, Benjamin. They had gone about a mile when there was a sudden snap and a violent shock in the car in which they were riding. The car swerved, swayed, and then toppled off the embankment, crashing into a field below.

In the midst of smashed seats and broken glass, Pierce, feeling dazed, sat up and looked for Jane. She was struggling to her feet, and he was thankful that she, too, seemed unhurt. Then to his horror, just a few yards away he saw Benjamin lying lifeless. Quickly, he went to his son, but there was nothing he could do. Benjamin was dead. Jane began to sob uncontrollably, and Pierce took her into his arms to comfort her.

After much soul-searching, Pierce's grieving wife came to believe that God had taken their last son so that her husband could give all his attention to being President. This cruel interpretation of the tragedy devastated Franklin Pierce's peace of mind as he was about to take office. As one biographer wrote in his book about Pierce, "His was not a frame of mind to command success or invite inspiration. Much of the difficulty which he experienced in administration during the next four years may be attributed to this terrible tragedy and its long continuing after effects."

PRESIDENT PIERCE

Despite his victory over Scott by more than 200,000 votes, Pierce knew the nation was pretty evenly divided between Democrats and Whigs. He also felt great responsibility for the ever-deepening chasm between the North and South over the slavery issue. And his wife, who had always been in fragile health, was a constant worry to him now. She had broken down completely after Benjamin's death, making it difficult for the newly elected President to keep his mind on public affairs.

But Pierce knew he had to put personal tragedy behind him and force himself to go on. So he set about his first duty—to select a competent Cabinet (his group of top advisors). His aim was to include men, whether or not they had been loyal to him, who reflected all viewpoints in the nation. His only criteria were that they accept the Compromise of 1850 as the law of the land and the principles of the Democratic Party platform (its position on issues). By making wise choices, Pierce hoped to show he was the "great ruler" that Nathaniel Hawthorne said he could be.

Choosing a Cabinet

Pierce was bombarded with suggestions for Cabinet positions by prominent Democrats who had helped him get elected. A great deal of consulting and negotiations took place before he selected the Cabinet that he hoped would bring the Democratic Party and the nation together. As secretary of state, Pierce chose William L. Marcy, a New Yorker. Jefferson Davis, a Mississippian, was named secretary of war. Marcy and Davis, in the two most important Cabinet posts, symbolized the unification of the North and South.

Pierce chose James Guthrie of Kentucky to be secretary of the treasury and James C. Dobbin of North Carolina for secretary of the Navy—two more men from the South to please the southern states. James Campbell of Pennsylvania was made postmaster general, and Robert McClelland of Michigan was given the post of secretary of the interior. General Caleb Cushing, an attorney from Massachusetts who had worked with other Mexican-American War generals for Pierce's nomination, was named attorney general.

Although it was to be a "compromise" Cabinet, every man Pierce selected had strong opinions—not one was a compromiser. He had also managed to include all the factions in the Democratic Party with the exception of Stephen A. Douglas of Illinois, an omission Pierce was to regret later on.

Back to Washington

Before he left for the nation's capital, President-elect Pierce went to Boston to be with his wife, who was still in shock over their son's death. Because Jane did not have the strength to face Washington yet, she would stay with relatives until after the inauguration. After a few days, Pierce gave Jane flowers and a bracelet, then sadly said good-bye. He wanted to stay longer with her, but he was to be President of the United States, and now he had other responsibilities.

After Pierce arrived in Washington, he had dinner with President Fillmore at the White House and then went on a whirl of social activities that included attending a wedding and inspecting a new ship. While working on his inaugural speech, the President-elect met dozens of people who were looking for jobs. All this activity was tiring for Pierce, who was still grieving for his son and nervous about taking over the presidency.

Jane arrived in nearby Baltimore on March 1. When Pierce visited her there, he found her in a worse frame of mind than ever before. She had been told that her husband had been working for the presidential nomination all along while allowing her to think he did not want it. Although this was not exactly true, Pierce returned to Washington feeling guiltier than ever.

The Inauguration

On March 4, 1853, at noon, President-elect Franklin Pierce rode with President Fillmore and two senators to the Capitol in an open carriage for the inaugural ceremony. Despite snow and a sharp wind, thousands lined Pennsylvania Avenue to catch a glimpse of the new President. Pierce, warmed by their cheers, stood and raised his hat.

In the Senate chamber from which he had retired 15 years earlier, before members of Congress, the Supreme Court, and the diplomatic corps, Franklin Pierce became the 14th President of the United States. Chief Justice Taney of the Supreme Court administered the oath of office. Because Vice-President-elect King was ill in Cuba, he was not there to be inaugurated.

President Pierce's inaugural address, given completely from memory, rang out in resonant tones. He began by saying, "It is a relief to feel that no heart but my own can know the personal regret and bitter sorrow over which I have been borne to a position so suitable for others rather than desirable for myself." He went on to speak in favor of national expansion, for peace, opening new trade channels, and economy in government.

Then Pierce came to the subject that worried the nation the most. After avowing his love for the Union, he said that slavery had been sanctioned by the Constitution. "I believe that it stands like any other admitted right, and that the states where it exists are entitled to efficient remedies to enforce the constitutional provisions." He continued, "I hold the laws of 1850, commonly called the 'Compromise Measures,' are strictly constitutional and to be unhesitatingly carried into effect." He concluded by saying that the nation had come safely through a perilous crisis, and he hoped it would be the end of the slavery question.

On March 4, 1853, Franklin Pierce was inaugurated as the 14th President of the United States. His wife was ill and could not attend the ceremony. Pierce (in the center with his left hand on his chest) gave his inaugural address completely from memory. (Library of Congress.)

Following the inauguration, there was a reception for Pierce at the White House. Because he was in mourning, the inaugural ball had been cancelled, making the reception the only opportunity the public would have to greet the new President. After many hours of handshaking, the well-wishers finally left the President and his private secretary, Sidney Webster, alone in welcome silence.

Later that evening, when Pierce went up to the President's living quarters, he found the rooms in complete disorder. Wearily, he found a bed and was soon alone with his thoughts. He was the President of the United States now, but he was not feeling much satisfaction. He was lonely for his wife and wished with all his heart that Benjamin could have been there to share his glory.

SETTLING IN AT THE WHITE HOUSE

The next day, President Pierce began to find his way around the White House. The damp, badly heated Executive Mansion (its official name) consisted of two stories and a basement, 31 rooms in all. On the first floor there were many worn public rooms, but Congress had just voted money to refurbish them. Pierce selected his office from one of three rooms designated for official business in the southeast area of the second floor. Here, seated at the desk that once belonged to Andrew Jackson, the President would receive callers, preside over Cabinet meetings, confer with congressmen, and handle all business matters.

Webster, who had a small private office nearby, was Pierce's only assistant. Later, Congress appointed Benjamin French to the White House. His job was to sign the President's name to documents validating the government's numerous land grants.

Pierce moved his personal belongings to the family residence on the other side of the second floor. It boasted a recently installed bathroom with one of the few bathtubs in Washington.

By the time Mrs. Pierce arrived in Washington two weeks later, the White House staff had everything under control. Jane was still in a deep depression. She stayed in her room most of the time, thinking about her son, even writing him letters. There was very little social activity at the White House, and although people thronged there to see the President, Mrs. Pierce was often unavailable.

Franklin Pierce, always a moody man, had come to Washington tired and dispirited. His sorrow, the heavy responsibility of being President, and the Washington climate combined to undermine his health. News reached Washington that Vice-President King had died on April 19, about the same time that rumors were circulating that the President was ill. Pierce had malaria, and in June cancelled all appointments. But, for the most part, he continued to carry on his presidential duties.

Appointments to Office

After Congress had accepted President Pierce's Cabinet, he was determined to make these seven men of differing opinions and backgrounds into a cohesive unit. He met with them every day, and with their help, made about 700 appointments to office. There were thousands of applicants. With every one, in addition to his qualifications for the job, the Cabinet had to consider the person's home state and his views on slavery.

Pierce changed this and decided to make the sole criterion for appointments the man's willingness to accept the Democratic Party platform. He passed over friends he thought unqualified and kept a Whig, John Wilson, in the land office because he was good at his job. But his old friend, Nathaniel Hawthorne, was made consul at Liverpool, England – a reward for the magnificent biography about Pierce that he had written. Pierce also appointed James Buchanan as minister to England, a post that was to make him a strong presidential candidate in the next election.

FOREIGN AFFAIRS

After being busy during his first months in office with politics and patronage (giving jobs to friends and political associates), other matters were brought to Pierce's attention. Secretary of State Marcy informed the President that there were three major trouble spots where U.S. interests seemed to be in danger: Great Britain, Mexico, and Spain. Great Britain claimed that the Clayton Bulwer Treaty of 1850 had not settled all issues between the United States and England in Central America. (The treaty gave both countries an equal share in the protection of a canal to be built in Central America. They also agreed to maintain the neutrality of the Central American country and the land on either side, nor would they attempt to control or fortify it.) This treaty kept the United States from building its own canal across Panama.

Although Britain had also agreed not to extend its financial interests in Latin America, Marcy had reports that the British were not living up to their agreement. And there were differences between the two countries about fishing rights off the Canadian coast.

As for Mexico, although the peace treaty ending the Mexican-American War had been signed in 1848, there were still many boundary disputes. Rival American-backed Mexican businessmen wanted U.S. State Department support for their claims that they had the right of way over the Isthmus of Tehuantepec. Then, Governor Lane of New Mexico issued a proclamation that the Mesilla Valley, one of the boundaries in dispute, belonged to his state. When Mexican President Santa Anna protested, Pierce decided to support Lane's claim. But he ordered the governor not to take possession of the valley until the government could negotiate the matter.

James Gadsden, a South Carolina railroad promoter, was named minister to Mexico. He was sent to negotiate for some territory south of New Mexico so a Southern Pacific Railroad route could be built there. Other orders included securing a release from U.S. obligations to protect Mexicans from Indian raids and attempting to improve trade relations with Mexico. When Gadsden reported that Santa Anna needed money and was ready to sell some land, the President and Secretary Marcy sent a negotiator to Mexico. His secret instructions were to offer $50 million for an area that included much of northern Mexico and all of the southern part of California.

The third problem Marcy brought to the President for consideration was that of Spain and Cuba. Earlier administrations had tried to buy Cuba and had offered as much as $100 million to the Spanish government. All offers had been refused. Since then, certain Americans who had been trying to get rich by creating troubles in Latin America (such people were called filibusters) had made the Spanish angry by saying they would attack Cuba and set it free. Pierce secretly hoped that with a little encouragement from the United States, Cuba—like Texas—would revolt against Spain and ask to be admitted to the Union as a state.

Trade expansion to Hawaii and other Pacific islands, as well as to the mainland of Asia, also interested the United States. Commodore Matthew Perry had been sent by a previous administration to establish trade relations with Japan. Now Pierce and Marcy wanted to open China as well. They sent an envoy to China to negotiate a two-way free trade agreement—with authority to use Perry's naval fleet, if necessary, to make the Chinese agree.

The Koszta Affair

In July 1853, in what was called the "Koszta Affair," Pierce's administration made a move that was widely acclaimed in the United States. Martin Koszta, a native of Austro-Hungary, was a resident of the United States and had declared his intention of becoming a citizen. That summer, while visiting Smyrna, a city in Turkey, he was arrested for having taken part in revolutionary activities in 1848. The Austrians were holding him aboard a warship that was to take him to Vienna to stand trial.

When Koszta asked the United States for protection, there was a U.S. naval vessel, the *St. Louis,* in Smyrna harbor at the time. The vessel's captain, Duncan Ingraham, threatened to fire on the Austrian ship unless Koszta was released to him. Instead, the Austrians turned Koszta over to the French consul at Smyrna and then sent a letter of protest to President Pierce, calling Captain Ingraham's action an outrage. Pierce and Secretary Marcy reviewed the evidence and replied in a letter to the Austrians that they upheld Captain Ingraham. In September, when the exchange of letters was revealed, Americans applauded the President for his decisive action.

Trouble with the Press

But there was not much more applause for President Pierce. As soon as he took office, he was in trouble with the press — mostly because of disappointed office-seekers. After Pierce had appointed John Mason as minister to France, James Bennett, the editor of the *New York Herald* who had wanted the job, criticized the President in his paper. And Francis Grund, a correspondent for the *Philadelphia Public Ledger* and the *Baltimore Sun,* who had wanted a consular position but did not get it, joined in the criticism.

Longtime Democrats were grumbling about Pierce's Cabinet selections, too, mainly because some qualified Democrats had been passed over. Attorney General Caleb Cushing had, until recently, been an abolitionist Whig. Others said Secretary of War Jefferson Davis was against the Union and did not merit his post. And there were those who criticized Secretary of State William Marcy because of his opposition to certain Democratic Party factions in New York. Also among the disgruntled were staunch Union men who objected to all southerners in office, and then there were southern extremists who were against everyone. There was no Cabinet that could have satisfied all factions of the Democratic Party.

Pierce did not ignore the criticism. He fought back by

encouraging friends to take over the *Union,* a Washington newspaper. After that, other editors called it propaganda whenever an article favorable to the Pierce administration appeared in the *Union.*

Seeking a Better Image

Hoping to improve his image, Pierce went to Philadelphia and met with Buchanan and other Democrats. He then went on to New York City to attend the first World's Fair. It rained while Pierce spoke at the fair, forcing him to ride his horse under an umbrella in the parade. Then, extremely tired, and because he had a cold, he drank a little too much brandy. This was promptly noted in a letter to Buchanan by one of the men in the presidential party.

President Pierce's New York trip did not do much to help his image. Now aided by a hostile press, the anti-Pierce rebellion had spread to New Hampshire, where even his friends were saying that Pierce was soft on their enemies. The fragmented Democratic Party was engaged in a tug of war, and sectionalism (North versus South) was the rope pulling it and the country apart.

Undaunted, President Pierce spoke of his vision for the United States in the future. It would become a large nation, he prophesied, that would endure only if the principle of states' rights was firmly guaranteed. He saw, in the movement westward and in the expansion of trade, a solution to the country's problems. If there were peace and prosperity, Americans would be unified. The President was optimistic that a friendly Congress would rally behind him when his legislative program was presented, and things would still work out well for him.

Chapter 8
Coping with Rivalries

In the beginning of 1854, Americans were pressing the Pierce administration to open more western territories to settlers so new states could be formed and eventually join the Union. But the President was not anxious to see this happen, because the slavery issue was bound to come up and create more problems for him. So he tried to divert public attention away from slavery by focusing on such foreign affairs as the purchase of Cuba, settling the Mexican border disputes, increasing trade with Latin America, and expanding trade across the Pacific.

Playing it safe, the President announced that the main thrust of his domestic policy was to fight the dishonesty and waste in government that remained after four years of the Whigs being in power. On the sensitive subject of states' rights versus human rights over the slavery issue, Pierce maintained that the Compromise of 1850 had permanently resolved the question of slavery in the states. But the President did not realize how strong the drive to expand to the West was, and the havoc it would bring.

This portrait of Franklin Pierce was made while he was serving as President of the United States. Pierce hoped to be the great ruler that Nathaniel Hawthorne said he could be. But the controversy over slavery became more and more crucial during his presidency, and Pierce had a difficult time holding the country together. (Library of Congress.)

THE 33RD CONGRESS

When the 33rd Congress met in December 1853, the Democrats were in control of both Houses. At first it seemed that Pierce's vision of a friendly Congress rallying behind his programs would materialize after all. But because the Democratic Party of 1853 was loosely held together by compromises, it could not be counted on to support the President.

Two weeks before Congress was to meet, Pierce received some bad news. Senator Charles G. Atherton of New Hampshire, the President's trusted spokesman in the Senate, had died. With the Great Triumvirate—Clay, Webster, and Calhoun—also gone, men of all factions were vying to fill their shoes. One who emerged as a Senate leader was the "Little Giant" from Illinois, Senator Stephen A. Douglas, a shrewd opportunist who was involved in western expansion, railroad development, and land speculation. Douglas had failed in his quest for the Democratic presidential nomination in 1852, and had been further disappointed by not being named to Pierce's Cabinet.

Early Problems

The President's first State of the Union message showed his optimism, yet it underscored his lack of leadership. He was not going to lead Congress, he said, but he was going to state "an orthodox Democratic President's creed" whereby the nation would live by the word of the Constitution. He thought the founding fathers had created a perfect instrument, and nobody could better it, nor should they try. The message showed that Pierce had no new ideas. He was no more innovative as the Chief Executive than he had been as a congressman.

Another problem came up for Pierce and his Cabinet

that had troubled several other administrations. Because of the brisk sale of public lands, there was a surplus of money in the U.S. Treasury. This meant that a lot of the cash in the nation was in government vaults and not available for use. Congress was besieged with schemers who flocked to Washington with ideas for using the money. Likewise, the prospect of new federal buildings and hospitals, as well as river and harbor improvements, caused the capital to be inundated by men seeking public works contracts.

To relieve the pressure on Congress, Pierce and Treasury Secretary James Guthrie decided to prepare a bill to lower tariffs (the taxes on imported goods), thereby reducing the amount of money the government collected. When the Army and Navy asked for federal funds to expand, Pierce agreed, again cutting the treasury surplus. The President also approved spending for a reorganization program for the backlogged federal courts.

THE KANSAS-NEBRASKA FIGHT

Enterprising men who wanted to build railroads to the Pacific Ocean asked the government for land grants and financial aid. Pierce favored land grants, but he believed that the building of railroads was up to the private business sector. Congress had passed laws providing for railroad surveys and for the breaking of treaties with Indians who were living on the lands the railroads wanted. Commissioner George W. Manypenny, head of the Office of Indian Affairs, was already in Kansas arranging for the seizure of such Indian lands.

Although the Pierce administration declared that the western territories were not yet open for settlement, Americans knew that it would not be long before they were. When Congress met in December 1853, members of both Houses brought bills to organize the Nebraska Territory. The bills were then sent to the Committee on Territories of each House. Senator Douglas, chairman of the Committee on Territories in the Senate, had a personal interest in the territorial bill he introduced on January 4.

Douglas' bill provoked a great deal of southern opposition. Senator David Atchison of Missouri, Acting Vice-President after Vice-President King died, said that any bill he would vote for must first provide for the repeal of the Missouri Compromise of 1820, which restricted slavery in the northwestern part of the Louisiana Purchase. Southerners, he said, did not agree that the Compromise of 1850 had settled the matter of which territories would be free and which ones would permit slavery. For southerners, the only way the issue would ever be settled was to leave it up to the people of the territories involved to decide how they wanted to live.

Influencing Congress

Stephen Douglas very much wanted congressional approval of his bill. So he took a long, hard look at the makeup of Congress to help him decide how to get it. In the House of Representatives, there were 158 Democrats and 72 Whigs. The Senate was composed of 37 Democrats, 22 Whigs, and two Free-Soilers. Douglas concluded that he needed the South if there was to be westward expansion. Furthermore, if the West and South joined forces, they would be strong enough to control congressional legislation. Although most southerners did not like or trust Douglas, he was the real leader of the Democrats in the Senate, and he had all the young Democrats behind him. There were also several western senators who owed loyalty to Douglas.

Control of the southerners was in the hands of a few powerful men. Atchison, who was next in line for the presidency if Pierce should die in office, was the most influential. When Atchison told Douglas that he wanted a repeal of the Missouri Compromise and its restrictions on slavery in the territories, Douglas knew he would never get the abolitionists to agree to it. But because the southerners were powerful and he had to cooperate with them to get his bill through, he found a more indirect way.

Douglas drew up a new bill to divide the territories of Kansas and Nebraska with the same wording that had been used to organize the territories of Utah and New Mexico. This gave the territorial legislatures all powers of legislation consistent with the Constitution. Slavery in the territories would be decided by their own courts. New states would be taken into the Union "with or without slavery," depending on what the people wanted at the time of admission. Because both the Kansas and Nebraska territories were north of the line that had been established between freedom and slavery, the bill went around the Missouri Compromise.

A Sunday Meeting

As far as is known, President Pierce was not consulted about Douglas' bill. The *Union* endorsed it, and Pierce accepted it because it was practically the same as the Compromise of 1850. And it agreed with the Baltimore platform of the Democratic Party. Besides, the President had always thought the Missouri Compromise to be unconstitutional.

It was a well-planned scheme, but a southern Whig, Archibald Dixon, ruined Douglas' bill by attaching an amendment specifically repealing (revoking) the slavery restriction in the Missouri Compromise. Southern Democrats had to go along with this provision because the people in their home states demanded it. Then, to make matters worse, Senator Charles Sumner from Massachusetts added another amendment to put back the Missouri Compromise restriction on slavery. Once again, the slavery conflict had been revived.

Trying to calm things down, Pierce's Cabinet proposed their own amendment that would limit the rights of persons and property to the restrictions of the Constitution and the courts. But the southerners refused it, firmly demanding the repeal of the Missouri Compromise.

Douglas was frantic. His bill was to come up on Monday, which was the next day. He had only 24 hours to convince the President to withdraw the Cabinet's amendment and accept Douglas' proposal as an administration bill. But President Pierce never did business on Sunday. So Douglas asked Jefferson Davis to persuade Pierce to make an exception and see him. Davis did so, Douglas was granted permission, and he brought five prominent congressmen to a meeting at the White House.

After an intense discussion Pierce saw the problem clearly. He had pledged that he would never reopen the slavery controversy, and he was also pledged to the Compromise of 1850. But he was in conflict with powerful senators, who must confirm his appointees and ratify (approve) treaties.

To a great extent, the success of Pierce's foreign policy depended on Senate approval. The men at the meeting wanted his assent to repeal a law he had always said was unconstitutional, and to substitute a principal upon which he was elected. It was a matter of practical politics. Pierce finally agreed. When Douglas asked that Pierce put his approval in writing, the President wrote a statement to the effect that "the Missouri Compromise was superseded by the principles of the legislation of 1850, commonly called the Compromise Measures, and is hereby declared inoperative and void." The statement went on to say that "people [of a territory or state are left] perfectly free to form and regulate their domestic institutions in their own way." The next day, the amended bill was presented to Congress. It was the first major fight of his administration, and Pierce, who had vowed never to take sides, was now deeply committed to one side.

Struggling to Pass a Bill

On January 24, 1854, Senator Charles Sumner, Senator Salmon P. Chase, and others who believed in the Missouri Compromise put out an "Appeal to the Independent Democrats." It called the Douglas bill a "gross violation of a sacred pledge," and charged that Pierce had sold out to the southerners.

For three months the Senate was locked in bitter debate. President Pierce was attacked by the *New York Tribune* and abolitionist papers. He was also in serious trouble with northern Democrats. Somehow he had to convince them to support the bill as a test of their loyalty to the Democratic Party. He used all his powers of persuasion and on March 3, when the measure was finally put to a vote, the Kansas-Nebraska bill passed 37 to 14.

Logrolling in the House

The next step was to get the Kansas-Nebraska bill through the House of Representatives. But it became bogged down in political "logrolling" (the trading of votes by one member on a project he did not care about for another member's vote on a project he wanted). At that time there were several other bills under consideration. Because all these bills represented conflicting interests, getting the House's approval of the Kansas-Nebraska bill became a matter of trade-offs.

As the House debated and traded votes, the Emigrant Aid Society was formed in Massachusetts to promote anti-slavery in Kansas when the territory became a state. The idea was for antislavery people to move into Kansas and outnumber their opponents. Not to be outdone, southern groups secretly promoted the movement of slaveholders and their slaves into Kansas for the same reason. Pressure was building for Pierce.

Nothing much happened for a while. Pierce watched and waited, but he was confident that the bill would pass the House by a majority of at least 20 and possibly 40 votes. In late March, however, the President was shocked to hear that there was a motion to commit the Kansas-Nebraska bill to the Committee of the Whole instead of the Committee on Territories. This move could kill the bill because of the former committee's full agenda.

When this happened, Pierce and his Cabinet sprang into action to keep the Kansas-Nebraska bill from being defeated. They argued, exerted pressure on congressmen, and used all their influence to persuade dissenters. Then they maneuvered to postpone 18 bills that stood in the way of their bill. At last, after bitter floor fights and a final 36-hour session, the disputed measure passed 113 to 100.

Pierce, his Cabinet, and Senator Douglas were victorious, but they had failed to get their party behind them. Only 100 of 159 House Democrats had voted for the bill. It was carried with the help of the 13 southern Whigs. On May 30, 1854, when President Pierce signed what he thought was his first great bill into law, known as the Kansas-Nebraska Act, he expressed the hope that the slavery question had been settled forever.

Chapter 9

Disappointments and Defeats

During the summer of 1854, doubt began to creep into Pierce's mind as to whether he was going to be strong enough as President to lead the country. Up until that time, he had successfully convinced congressmen to get behind him in order to pass the measures that he wanted. He had enlarged the Navy, increased Army pay, and passed several treaties. He had also vetoed (rejected) a few bills, and his vetoes had been sustained.

But Pierce's popularity was dwindling, and he knew it. On the last afternoon of the congressional session, after signing several bills, he was ready to leave the Capitol building. Walking into the rotunda to await his carriage, the President was met by a drunken young man who insisted that he have a drink with him. To Pierce, liquor always meant trouble, so he refused. Yet the fellow kept urging Pierce to join him for a drink. When his carriage arrived, the President turned his back to get in and the young man hit him with a hard-boiled egg. The egg-thrower was arrested, but Pierce later withdrew the charges. This assault demonstrates how people were beginning to feel about the Pierce administration.

A VIGOROUS FOREIGN POLICY

One of the foundations of Pierce's foreign policy was the belief, strengthened by his advisors, that France and Britain were working together against American interests. Actually, they worked against the United States only when American interests conflicted with theirs, as, for example, in Latin America.

President Pierce dreamed of a vigorous foreign policy, but his ideas were way ahead of their time. His first attempt at diplomacy abroad began when he sent James Gadsden of South Carolina to Mexico to settle the ongoing boundary dispute between the two countries. A few days before the Sunday conference with Senator Douglas on the Kansas-Nebraska bill, Gadsden sent home his completed treaty. It included a payment to Mexico of $15 million for about 30,000 square miles of territory in the Mesilla Valley, in what are now the states of Arizona and New Mexico.

The President was not satisfied with the treaty. He expected more land for so large a sum of money, and besides, Gadsden had not settled all the territorial claims. Pierce and his advisors debated the matter for a month, then they sent the treaty to the Senate with several amendments. After reducing the payment for the land to $10 million, the treaty with Mexico was finally ratified in June of 1854. To Pierce, the Gadsden Purchase, as the treaty with Mexico came to be called, was the first step in territorial expansion that was to make the United States a world power.

The Attempt to Buy Cuba

In the spring of 1854, Spanish authorities in Cuba seized the cargo of the American vessel *Black Warrior.* They claimed the ship had violated the rules of the port of Havana. American newspapers provoked the public into demanding that U.S. warships be sent to Havana. It was Pierce's first international crisis, and the issue was debated at many Cabinet meetings. The President blamed England and France for goading Spain into action against the United States.

Secretary of State Marcy demanded an apology from Spain, citing 16 cases of insults to Americans in Cuban waters. Then Marcy learned that Spain was on the verge of a revolution and that Cuba might be for sale. Because England and France were involved in Europe with the Russo-Turkey War, it was the perfect time for the United States to make such a deal with the Spanish. On April 3, Marcy told the American minister to Spain, Solon E. Borland, to begin negotiations to buy Cuba. (The next day Marcy also drew up plans to purchase Alaska from the Russians, and soon after, he planned to annex Hawaii. A vigorous foreign policy was truly under way.)

When it became known that Pierce was interested in purchasing Cuba, General John Quitman, a well-known filibuster, announced that he was organizing an expedition in New Orleans to "free" Cuba from the Spanish. To help him, Senator John Slidell of Louisiana made a motion in the Senate that the neutrality laws of the United States be suspended for a year to allow the filibusters to invade Cuba. The southern senators did not like the idea because they had heard that the new government that had been formed in Spain might free all slaves owned by Spaniards, and that would create a new problem at their doorstep.

Since the debate over the Kansas-Nebraska bill was still going on, the President was not anxious to stir up more talk about slavery. And it did not make sense for Secretary Marcy to carry on negotiations with Spain to buy Cuba if filibusters were going to be allowed to take over the island. So Pierce issued a proclamation to stop the Quitman expedition. But negotiations with Spain broke down anyway because Congress would not approve the money to buy Cuba.

Then August Belmont, an American banker, suggested that the President make other arrangements to buy Cuba through private European bankers. So Pierce continued to negotiate. Unwisely, however, he told people what he was doing. As word got around Europe, the Spanish government cut off negotiations with the United States for fear of other nations interpreting the sale of Cuba as being a sign of weakness.

Settling British and American Fishing Rights

During the last days of the struggle over the Kansas-Nebraska bill, while Pierce was working on his Cuban policy, the British Governor General of Canada, Lord Elgin, came to Washington to settle an old dispute concerning American and British fishing rights along the Atlantic coast. Secretary Marcy and Elgin soon signed a treaty granting fishing privileges to the United States along coastal inlets in the Canadian provinces of New Brunswick, Nova Scotia, Quebec, and Prince Edward Island. In turn, the British won the right to fish along the U.S. coastline down to the 36th parallel. President Pierce was pleased with the treaty. He thought of it as the first step in what eventually could be a peaceful merger of the United States and Canada.

The Greytown Affair

In the meantime, problems in Central America were aggravated by Minister Borland's hostility to Great Britain. He proceeded to negotiate a treaty guaranteeing territory to Nicaragua that Great Britain already occupied. The horrified administration put the treaty aside and granted Borland's request that he be recalled (removed from his position). But before he left Nicaragua, the minister took part in what came to be known as the Greytown Affair, which stemmed from Commodore Cornelius Vanderbilt's business interests.

Since the days of the California gold rush in 1848 and 1849, American firms had established steamship lines down the East Coast of the United States to Panama and Nicaragua. They then ran stagecoaches and trains across the isthmus to the Pacific Ocean, where ships sailed from Nicaragua and Panama up to San Francisco. One such firm was Vanderbilt's Accessory Transit Company, constantly in trouble with British authorities at Greytown, Nicaragua (England supposedly governed Nicaragua as a "protectorate" over the Mosquito Indians, but in reality the country was a British dependency).

Vanderbilt had angered the British earlier when he had said he would build his own canal across Nicaragua. Then, just before Borland left Nicaragua, one of the captains of a Vanderbilt ship was arrested for murder. When U.S. Minister Borland intervened to help the captain, the American public applauded his action, thereby further aggravating Great Britain.

The Ostend Manifesto

Despite problems with the British over Nicaragua and other matters, Pierce still had not given up hope of purchasing Cuba from Spain. In October of 1854, Secretary Marcy authorized Pierre Soule, the American minister to Spain, to confer with John Mason, the country's minister to France, and James Buchanan, the U.S. minister to Britain, about acquiring Cuba. The men met at Ostend, Belgium, for three days and then spent six days at another location. On October 18, they signed a dispatch, later known as the Ostend Manifesto, which said that Cuba was important to American interests, especially slavery, and indicated that if the United States could not buy Cuba, then the country should take it by force.

The three ministers pretended to be afraid that a slave rebellion would turn Cuba into an unruly black republic. But the Manifesto went too far, even for American public opinion. When all political parties condemned it, the last hope for acquiring Cuba was gone. The country thought Pierce was at fault. But the President blamed Congress for not voting him the money to make the purchase.

Wheeling and Dealing for Expansion

There were other disappointments in Pierce's expansion program. In November 1854, the State Department received a treaty from Hawaii for the immediate admission of the Kingdom of Hawaii to the Union as a state. Because the British and French governments were opposed to such annexation, and because congressional approval was also uncertain, the treaty was sent back to Hawaii for revision.

In the meantime, the Hawaiian king had died, so all annexation negotiations were ended. It seemed that in whatever direction the President turned, his expansion policy would either meet with disapproval from European countries or Congress would let him down.

The reason Congress did not go along with Pierce's expansion ideas was because of the Kansas-Nebraska Act, which had become the symbol of the slavery issue. Pierce had also made certain moves, such as his veto of an internal improvements bill in the summer of 1854, that angered western senators and representatives. Although Pierce had stuck by his principles that there should be no federal support for state or regional improvements, his hopes of going down in history as a strong President were beginning to fade.

OPPOSITION TO PIERCE AND THE DEMOCRATS

Although President Pierce had thought that when he signed the Kansas-Nebraska Act he had put an end to the slavery issue, he was wrong. Whigs, Democrats, Free-Soilers, and others had met in February 1854 at Ripon, Wisconsin, to talk about establishing a new political party to fight slavery. In July, at a meeting in Jackson, Michigan, politicians followed through on the meeting in Ripon and formed the Republican Party.

The first action of the Republicans was to demand an end to slavery in the District of Columbia and repeal of the Fugitive Slave Law. Pierce had dealt with these issues before, but he did not want them to come up now for fear they would bring on another sectional conflict. That summer, Republican meetings were held in other states. The battle cry beginning to be heard across the country was "Down with slavery!"

Although Pierce knew that some independent Democrats and other politicians were forming a new political movement that summer, he did not realize how strong it was. Washington was unbearably hot, so he went on a short vacation to Capon Springs, Virginia, with Jane, Jefferson Davis, and other friends. When he returned in September of that congressional election year, the President was optimistic about the Democrats winning a majority in Congress. But it bothered him to hear that there were now Democrats who wanted to defeat those in their own party who had voted for the Kansas-Nebraska bill.

The Know-Nothings

The Know-Nothing Party was another political organization that was gaining strength in New Hampshire and other eastern states. It was now out to capture the South, too. The party was anti-Catholic, calling for the exclusion of Catholics from public office. Because Pierce had appointed James Campbell, a Catholic, to his Cabinet as postmaster general, the Know-Nothings said he was under the thumb of the Catholic Church.

Marcy wrote to Pierce that the strength of the Know-Nothings would be tested in the congressional election in Virginia. If the Know-Nothings won, he warned, they might establish a successful, permanent party. Because the organization was based almost completely on prejudice, Pierce did everything he could to defeat their candidates. Happily, the Know-Nothings lost and the party went into a decline.

KANSAS AGAIN

Nothing much was accomplished during the winter congressional session of 1854–1855, due to a lack of leadership in Congress. The Army and Navy were again voted funds, and laws were passed to make travel on steamboats safer. A telegraph line to the Pacific was begun and homesteads were granted to veterans. But Pierce vetoed an appropriations bill to subsidize a failing steamship line that probably ruined American chances to increase its foreign trade. The nation was sluggish and uneasy. It may have been because of what was happening in Kansas.

To avoid partiality in the territories, Pierce decided to appoint a northerner to be governor of Kansas and a southerner to govern Nebraska. In June of 1854 he appointed Andrew H. Reeder of Pennsylvania to govern Kansas. Although Reeder was a competent man, he was without administrative experience and did not have the faintest notion about frontier life. As soon as the South heard about Reeder's appointment, they thought Pierce was going to turn Kansas into a free state.

Reeder took time to wind up his personal business and finally arrived in Fort Leavenworth, Kansas, in October. By then, matters had grown more complicated, making it almost impossible to figure out how to govern Kansas. Speculators, including Governor Reeder himself, had bought land as soon as the territory had been opened for settlement. The Emigrant Aid Society of New England was bringing in armed settlers from the North so Kansas would become a free territory. Missourians, led by Senator Atchison and other slaveholders, fought the Emigrant Aid Society by invading the territory and intimidating the inhabitants with their guns.

Squatters took over land belonging to the Delaware Indians and had to be driven off by federal troops. George Manypenny of the Office of Indian Affairs and other Indian agents were trying to protect the rights of Indians who were losing their lands to speculators and settlers.

By November, there was even more confusion. An election was held to elect a territorial delegate to Congress, and the southerners' candidate, John W. Whitfield, won by fraud. Alarmed by the election results, New Englanders sent more money to Kansas and brought in scores of armed men.

The President's Plan

In the meantime, protests from the Indian agents against Governor Reeder were on their way to Washington. He and his associates were charged with unlawful conduct and cheating the Indians in land deals. On March 30, 1855, local elections were held in Kansas to choose a territorial legislature, and a proslavery legislature was elected. In May, Governor Reeder went East to obtain political support. While in Pennsylvania, he made a speech charging that Missourians had seized the legislature fraudulently and had threatened him with force.

When Senator Atchison read an account of Reeder's speech, he was so angry that he made a special trip to Washington. He told the President about all of Reeder's wrongdoings and insisted that he be removed from office.

President Pierce thought it over. Granted, Reeder had not been the best governor, but he had tried to steer a middle course. Besides, he had many influential friends. To remove him would be giving in to southern demands.

So the President formed a plan. He took Reeder to task for his unlawful activities and then said he would overlook them. Next, Pierce invited the governor to resign, telling him that he was deeply concerned about his safety. Also, if Reeder went back to Kansas, it could bring on a civil war. When Reeder would not take the hint, Pierce bluntly asked him to resign. But Reeder refused. He said he had to return to Kansas to show the southerners that the federal government was behind him.

While all this was happening, Kansas was without a governor. In June Pierce reluctantly allowed Reeder to go back to Kansas and straighten out the mess. As soon as he returned, Reeder called a meeting of the territorial legislature at Pawnee City. He wanted to make Pawnee the territorial capital because he owned land in the area. The legislature fought against the site and moved out.

Noting the deadlock, Pierce finally removed Reeder and others involved in the Pawnee City transactions. The city was destroyed, and the site returned to the Indians. The South now pushed for a southerner to be governor. But Pierce, still trying to be impartial, chose Wilson Shannon, former governor of Ohio, who was a neutral on the slavery question. Kansas was to have another chance.

Chapter 10

A One-Term President

W hen writing his annual State of the Union message to Congress in December 1855, the President gave very little space to Kansas. He acknowledged there had been some trouble out West, but he said it was not serious enough for him to intervene. He would only do so, he said, "in case of obstruction to Federal law or of organized resistance to Territorial law assuming the character of insurrection." If these things did occur, he promised to take action promptly. Pierce had always believed in the limited powers of the Chief Executive. As the leader of his party, he thought he could save the Union by protecting constitutional rights.

A DISORGANIZED HOUSE

On December 3, 1855, when Congress met, the House failed to organize and the Democratic caucus nominee could not muster enough votes to be elected Speaker. It had never happened before. Now Pierce could not present his State of the Union message. The President received another blow when his old enemy from New Hampshire, John P. Hale, was returned to the Senate after a two-year absence. Those two events were bad enough, but the worst was yet to come. That same day, Pierce received a telegram from a shaken Governor Shannon in Kansas asking him to send federal troops to help him keep order. Pierce replied that he would do so when he was told all particulars of the situation. The next time Shannon wrote the President, a truce had been arranged between the two Kansas factions. It was not yet time to send in the troops.

Taking the Initiative

Pierce begged the House of Representatives to get itself organized and elect a Speaker. Delicate negotiations were taking place with Great Britain, and if the U.S. government was not functioning and his annual message could not be delivered, the British would think he had lost power to govern. But the House still did not elect a speaker. As the end of the year approached, Pierce was desperate. Finally, his advisors pointed out that if the House was not organized, the Senate was.

In an unprecedented move, Pierce bypassed the House and sent his annual message up to Capitol Hill, where it was read in the Senate. Not long after, Buchanan, the American minister in England, was instructed to demand the recall of the British ambassador for recruiting troops on American soil to fight for England in Europe. Pierce had finally taken the initiative, hoping his actions would impress Congress and the American people.

But Senator Hale was not impressed. Questioning the President's right to send his annual message to the Senate before the House was organized, he launched a bitter attack on Pierce's foreign and domestic policies on the Senate floor.

Pierce was a sociable person who liked parties and balls. When his wife, Jane, was up to it, the White House was the center of Washington's social activity, and crowds came and went through the gas-lit rooms. (Library of Congress.)

In Hale's opinion, the President's message was nothing but a bid for renomination. And, he concluded, Pierce had no more chance of being renominated than a Senate page.

Early in 1856, with Jane feeling better, the White House became the center of social activity. Crowds came and went through the gas-lit rooms as the Marine band played under the staircase. One evening, Senator Hale brought a group of people to meet the President. Turning his back on the Senator, Pierce greeted the others. This snub guaranteed a continuance of Hale's personal war with the President.

A TWO-GOVERNMENT TERRITORY

Much had happened in Kansas since Governor Reeder had been removed. After the quarrel between the governor and the legislature over Pawnee, the antislavery group claimed that the territorial government was no longer legal. The group met in September of 1855 and asked that Kansas be admitted to the Union as a free state.

The Emigrant Aid Society poured arms into Kansas for the "Free State" army, and James H. Lane became commander of its forces. Late in October a convention was called and Free Staters drew up what was called the "Topeka Constitution" prohibiting slavery but also keeping blacks out of the territory. It seemed that Kansas now had two governments, each with its own army. The President had no cause for optimism.

By the end of January 1856, the news from Kansas was alarming. The Antislavery group had elected their own governor and legislature in defiance of the territorial government. Fighting broke out. To add to the trouble, former Governor Reeder had been elected by the Free-Soilers to be the congressional representative of their government. Pierce called it revolution, but as the House still was not organized, there could be no laws passed.

In the hopes of swaying certain House members to unite and organize, Pierce sent them a message telling how grave the situation was in Kansas. As Chief Executive, he said, his duty was to uphold the properly elected territorial government against the rebellious "Topeka" government elected that fall. But sensing danger ahead, he made two recommendations to Congress. First, he called for an immediate constitutional convention to admit Kansas as a state. Second, he asked for a special appropriation to cover the cost of sending federal troops to Kansas.

Meeting the Crisis in Kansas

Nothing happened then because the House still had not elected a Speaker. But finally, in February, Republican Nathaniel Banks was elected. Instead of stabilizing the situation, however, Banks' election complicated matters more by making Kansas a political issue in Washington, too. On February 11, Pierce sent a message to Congress in which he said that he was still giving full support to the duly elected original territorial legislature in Kansas and that both the House and Senate were overreacting to the problem. This message deepened convictions that Pierce favored the South. But in the President's mind, he was a nationalist trying to uphold law and order and suppress treason.

Three days later, Kansas Governor Shannon arrived in Washington to confer with Pierce and Marcy. They sent him back to Kansas with instructions for Colonel Sumner, the commander of federal troops in Kansas, that Sumner was to put his troops at Shannon's disposal. Meanwhile, the Senate Committee on Territories, under Douglas, prepared a statehood bill. It was presented on March 12, authorizing Kansas to form a constitution and a state government as soon as the population reached 93,420 (the number of people that would entitle Kansas to have one congressman). Because there were only about 30,000 people living in Kansas then, this would postpone statehood for a while, leaving the region under control of the territorial legislature. A few days later, Douglas made a speech lauding the President for the promptness with which he had met the crisis in Kansas. Of course, not all members of the Senate agreed with Douglas. Pierce had played right into the hands of his enemies.

More Political Issues

Because of Douglas' statehood bill for Kansas, both proslavery and antislavery groups began sending more people into the territory. For the Republicans, Kansas became a major election issue, and they began stirring up resentment against the South. The difficulties in troubled Kansas were magnified in Congress for all the world to see. Newspapers reported every little incident as if the territory was swimming in blood. With hindsight, it is easy to see that Pierce made the wrong move at the time by giving his political enemies a perfect issue.

If Pierce had declared Kansas to be in crisis and had not encouraged statehood, things may have turned out differently. Strangely, the southerners thought that Pierce had created the whole problem in order that Kansas would be admitted to the Union as a free state. They blamed him for appointing Reeder as governor, and the North blamed Pierce for removing Reeder. Republicans called Pierce a weakling who had sold out to the South because he wanted to be re-elected.

FOREIGN AFFAIRS PROBLEMS

In the spring of 1856, foreign affairs were not going smoothly for Pierce either. While tangling with Great Britain about recruiting troops on American soil, the public had expected the President to do something spectacular. But the affair resulted in a tame climax that did not add to Pierce's reputation.

This group portrait shows President Pierce and his seven Cabinet members in discussion. Pierce conducted presidential affairs not as a leader, but as a member of his own Cabinet. (Library of Congress.)

In March, William Walker, an American filibuster, invaded war-torn Nicaragua with the support of Commodore Vanderbilt and the Accessory Transit Company. Walker seized the government and put in one of his own men as president. The American minister to Nicaragua recognized the new government immediately. But Pierce could not afford to support a violation of neutrality when he was hammering at Great Britain for the very same thing. So he and his Cabinet withdrew the recognition. In May, however, when the British refused to recall their ambassador for recruiting troops on U.S. soil, there was so much pressure on Pierce to do something against England that he finally agreed to recognize Walker's government.

NEW VIOLENCE IN KANSAS

Trouble with foreign affairs was nothing compared to what was going on at home in May 1856. It began when Sheriff Jones of Lawrence, Kansas, was shot. Shortly thereafter, Lawrence was sacked and burned and two were killed. The town was in a state of siege. On May 22, Preston Brooks, a southerner, forced his way onto the Senate floor and beat Senator Charles Sumner of Massachusetts so fiercely with a cane that it almost crippled him. Because of the attack, northern senators began wearing guns for protection.

On May 24, John Brown, an abolitionist, led the Pottawatomie Creek Massacre, killing five proslavery colonists near Dutch Henry's Crossing in Kansas. The next day, Kansas became an armed camp. All of this violence was the result of Pierce's Kansas-Nebraska policy.

THE DEMOCRATIC NATIONAL CONVENTION OF 1856

The first Democratic National Convention to be held in the West was about to begin in Cincinnati, Ohio, on June 2. The delegates, hearing about the violence in Kansas, knew that only a very strong candidate could bring party victory. Most Democrats linked both President Pierce and Senator Douglas with the troublesome Kansas-Nebraska Act. And the party was split over the Brooks-Sumner affair. Southerners said Senator Sumner had deserved the beating, given his bitter tirades in Congress against slaveholders and his insults to Brooks' uncle, Senator Andrew P. Butler from South Carolina. But northern members thought that Brooks had reacted too severely and were highly critical of his actions.

Between the situation in Kansas, the South versus the North in Congress, and the Pottawatomie Massacre, Pierce was not too popular when the convention began. He also did not help himself when he vetoed two internal improvement bills at that time. Still, he hoped to be nominated by his party for a second term.

Losing the Nomination

When the convention opened, the two-thirds rule was adopted. This meant that a candidate for the presidential nomination had to receive two-thirds (198) of the votes of all the delegates in order to win. In addition to Pierce, the other leading contenders for the nomination were James Buchanan and Stephen Douglas.

Pierce and Buchanan were favored by most southerners, but the North did not trust either of them because they were identified with the Kansas-Nebraska Act. Because Buchanan was the U.S. minister to England, he had been out of the country most of the time for the past few years, so little was known about his views on domestic policy.

Pierce did not attend the convention. He stayed in Washington reading the newspapers, visiting the Smithsonian Institution, and waiting. During the first three days of the convention, the party platform was adopted, incorporating the Kansas-Nebraska Act in principle. The fourth morning brought Pierce bad news. New York seats were split between two opposing delegations from the state. Pierce could not attain a majority of the New York delegates with both groups present.

On the first ballot that afternoon, Buchanan received 135 votes to 122 for Pierce. Douglas had 33 votes and there were 5 votes for Lewis Cass. Pierce had counted on getting 145 votes on the first ballot, but parts of the Kentucky, Massachusetts, and Ohio delegations had let him down. His greatest disappointment, however, was Virginia, the state whose votes had put him over the top in 1852. Buchanan was their man this time.

Ballot after ballot followed, and Pierce's chances were becoming slimmer with each ballot. On the sixth ballot, he lost Tennessee. On the next ballot, he lost Arkansas, Georgia, and Kentucky. Fourteen ballots were cast before the convention adjourned for the day. That night, the delegates worked behind the scenes going to meeting after meeting making deals. Finally, the President's supporters were forced to drop him in favor of Douglas.

The next morning at the convention, Pierce's name was withdrawn and most of his votes went to Douglas. The strategy was to block Buchanan and force a compromise candidate. But on the second ballot that day, Douglas received only 122 votes. The strategy failed, and Buchanan won the nomination.

A Painful Time

For Franklin Pierce, it was a painful time. He had received the nomination four years ago for the same reasons that Buchanan had just been nominated. But the Democratic Party now needed a man whose views on national affairs were not too well known, particularly his views on slavery in the territories. Because Buchanan had spent the last few troublesome years in England, he was the best choice to save the party.

Once Buchanan was nominated, the delegates tried to make up for their failure to renominate President Pierce by passing a resolution praising him:

Resolved: That the administration of Franklin Pierce has been true to the great interests of the country. In the face of the most determined opposition it has maintained the laws, enforced economy, fostered progress and infused integrity and vigor into every department of the government at home. It has signally improved our treaty relations, extending the field of commercial enterprise and vindicated the rights of American citizens abroad. It has asserted with eminent impartiality the just claims of every section and has at all times been faithful to the Constitution. We therefore proclaim our unqualified approbation of its measures and policy.

That Saturday night, Franklin Pierce, still bitterly disappointed, heard noises on the White House lawn. From an upper window he saw perhaps 5,000 people gathered, shouting and calling his name. He managed a smile and told them that he was in favor of the nomination of James Buchanan. Men, he said, are dwarfs—unimportant in the scheme of things when compared with principles, and President Franklin Pierce would always stand on principle.

A LAME DUCK PRESIDENT

Now Pierce faced the "lame duck" days, when the President had to continue to carry on his duties but knew that he would soon be out of office. Pierce did not want to leave any unfinished business for his successor, which meant solving the Kansas problem. Since the middle of May, the situation there had become even worse. After the December truce had been broken, Pierce sent many telegrams to warn authorities in Kansas that federal troops were to be used only if absolutely necessary to preserve order and enforce the law.

Because of the sacking of Lawrence and the Pottawatomie murders, people were of two different opinions. The Whigs and Buchanan forces wanted to send General Winfield Scott to Kansas to take charge of the federal troops. Others felt that it was the very presence of the soldiers that were causing the problems, and they wanted the troops withdrawn. As Commander-in-Chief, Pierce decided to send General Persifor F. Smith, a friend from the Mexican-American War and a good Democrat, to take command of the troops in Kansas.

Perhaps the most important result of the Kansas-Nebraska Act was the birth of the Republican Party. Strictly a party of the North, its formation showed how much ground antislavery sentiment had gained. At their national convention in Philadelphia, the Republicans nominated John C. Frémont as their candidate for President and used Pierce's mistakes with Kansas and the need for Kansas to be a free state in their party platform.

The Toombs Bill

The Democrats in Congress had hoped that one of their measures, the Toombs bill, might resolve the problems in Kansas. Under this bill, a census would be taken in Kansas and then an election would be held. Only voters who had lived in Kansas for three months or more when the census was taken would be eligible to vote. In that way, neither the North nor the South could send in squatters. Members would be elected to attend a constitutional convention, and they would then write a constitution for Congress to consider.

Pierce favored the Toombs bill because he thought it would preserve the principle of constitutionalism that he believed in. Northern Democrats favored it for the same reason. Southern Democrats liked it because they felt it was their last chance to make Kansas a slave state. Southerners who had visited Kansas felt there was some hope that the territory would vote for slavery if left alone.

The Senate passed the Toombs bill. But the hostile House, dominated by Whigs and Know-Nothings, said the President was under southern domination and never gave much thought to the bill. The confusion in Kansas had become a political power struggle over who would control the territory.

Civil War in Kansas

By now, the violence in Kansas had led to civil war. Several men had been arrested and indicted for treason in federal courts. Governor Shannon tried to keep order but failed. Pierce had been pressured since the Lawrence disaster to remove the governor, and at the end of July, he recalled Shannon and appointed John W. Geary of Pennsylvania to take his place.

But Pierce had only exchanged one problem for another. The anti-Democratic House of Representatives refused to allow the use of federal troops to restore order in Kansas. Noting that northern forces were winning the Kansas civil war, the House put an amendment on the Army appropriations bill that forbade the President to use federal troops to enforce the laws of any territorial legislature. The Senate refused to accept the House amendment. As a result, Congress adjourned without appropriating funds for the Army. Because the government did not have the money to send the Army to several other strategic places where troops were needed, Pierce issued a call for a special session of Congress to take place within three days. He was not about to let the Kansas issue destroy the U.S. Army.

Meanwhile, because the Army had no funds to pay its soldiers, armories were closed and men were laid off. Taking advantage of the situation, abolitionist James Lane and his army invaded Kansas. Then the Missourians threatened to come in with their army and fight Lane. Finally, after a week of voting at the special session, Congress stopped playing politics with the Army and passed an appropriations bill. When Congress adjourned for the second time, Governor Geary left for Kansas with instructions to preserve order but to remain neutral.

Pierce tried to avert open rebellion in Kansas by issuing specific instructions to the troops. Many mistakes had been made in the past, he acknowledged, but now with Geary and Smith in charge, things would be straightened out. Secretary of War Davis ordered the governors of Illinois and Kentucky to alert their militia if it became necessary to preserve order in Kansas.

General Smith managed to suppress open rebellion, although there were still small rebellions and many heavily armed men in the territory. On September 27, Pierce heard from Smith that he had peacefully turned back 1,000 armed Missourians who were marching toward Kansas to fight the Free-Soilers. Now Pierce was convinced that he had solved the problem and that peace would finally come to Kansas.

Chapter 11
Life After the White House

Some years later, the sad news of President Lincoln's assassination caused the people of Concord to call an emotional town meeting to publicly express their grief. They declared that every home must show a draped flag and that they would punish anyone who did not display one. Then someone in the crowd yelled Pierce's name and called him a traitor, and the excited throng marched toward the house of the former President of the United States.

One of Pierce's servants ran to warn him that a mob was on the way. The general rose from his sickbed, took a small flag, and went to the door, where the angry mob was screaming insults. His tormentors demanded a patriotic speech about Lincoln. Pierce began, condemning the assassination, when someone shouted, "Where is your flag?" Franklin Pierce pulled himself up proudly and said in his best orator's voice:

> It is not necessary for me to show my devotion for the Stars and Stripes by any special exhibitions. . . . If the period which I have served our state and country in various situations, commencing more that thirty-five years ago, has left the question of my devotion to the flag, the Constitution and the Union in doubt, it is too late now to resume it by any such exhibition as the inquiry suggests.

There was silence when Pierce finished, and the chastened crowd left. But the former President was shaken by the experience. When he had planned his retirement years before, he did not have a clue that one day he would be confronted by such an angry mob.

PLANS FOR RETIREMENT

It was in October 1856 that President Pierce went to Concord to plan for his retirement. His arrival was greeted by cheering throngs who lined the curbs to watch the President ride his horse down Main Street. Although most of his townspeople welcomed him, many former political friends did not. Later, when he returned to Washington, he was happy to see that control of Congress was once more in the hands of the Democrats.

Accomplishments While President

Looking ahead, Pierce thought Buchanan should have a relatively easy time as President. Kansas was quiet, and principle had won. All Pierce had to do before he actually left Washington was to work with his Cabinet on his final reports. The government had given away almost 94 million acres of land. This helped to extend land ownership westward and to consolidate the American continent.

Although pensions and patents were in good shape, Pierce made suggestions for improvements in the pension system and advised Congress to revise the outgrown patent system. The work of the Indian Bureau had doubled in the last four years, and 52 treaties had been signed. The national debt had been reduced to $31 million, but the federal surplus continued. For the fourth time, the administration asked Congress for a reduction in tariffs so as to reduce government income.

The Army had done a good job quelling Indian upris-
ings and restoring law and order in Kansas "without shed-
ding one drop of blood." The Navy was opening roads to trade,
and six new frigates were almost completed. Although the
post office had a large deficit, it had greatly extended mail
service, especially by railroad.

As for foreign affairs, for the moment at least, all problems with Great Britain had been settled. Britain and America were negotiating a treaty to guarantee the safety of the
Mosquito Indians on the east coast of Central America. And
Greytown—where there had been so much trouble—was to
become a free port. Moreover, Great Britain was leaving Nicaragua and Honduras in accordance with the demands of the
Pierce administration. William Walker, however, was still in
power in Nicaragua, but Pierce could do nothing about it at
that time.

Last Days of the Presidency

Late in November of 1856, Pierce became ill while working
on his final State of the Union address. Then more trouble
came from Kansas when Governor Geary charged Chief Justice Lecompte of the territorial courts and two of his aides
with improper conduct in regard to bail. Pierce got rid of
Lecompte's two friends, and he tried but failed to dismiss the
judge and appoint a new one before he left office. As the year
ended, Kansas did quiet down and Pierce hoped that this peace
would be final. He did not know that Kansans were just waiting for the new administration to come in before they went
into action again.

Then on December 2, Senator Hale unleashed a blister-
ing verbal attack on Pierce. Returning on December 11 to
continue his attack on the President, Hale gleefully referred
to his speech of the previous January, when he predicted that
Pierce had no chance of being renominated. A number of

other congressmen spoke out against Pierce, too. Although some of his friends came to Pierce's defense, their speeches did not match the attacks in number or effectiveness.

The beginning of 1857 went by quickly. On February 24, Pierce held his last Tuesday afternoon reception. Then all of Washington turned out to say good-bye to the retiring President at a Friday evening gala. Although Pierce may have had enemies in the North and was a victim of partisan politics, he was personally very attractive and well liked.

The Final Departure

Amidst a flurry of last-minute details, March 3, 1857, arrived. It was now time for President Pierce and his wife to say farewell to the White House. Jane went to Secretary Marcy's home in Washington, where she and the President were going to stay until the weather in New Hampshire improved. The final Cabinet meeting was held, after which the President signed several new bills and spent his last night in the White House. The next day, before turning over the government to President James Buchanan, Pierce signed several more new bills. Then, after attending Buchanan's inauguration, he joined Jane at the Marcy home.

Franklin Pierce was now 52 years old. He had no financial worries because he had saved half of his presidential salary of $25,000 a year. At the end of his term, he had $78,000 that he had invested. Because he had no one to take care of except himself and Jane, the money was enough to live on. He loved his wife and wanted to spend time with her to make up for neglecting her while he was President for the last four years. Knowing how much she had hated the White House and living in Washington, he tried to help her lose the depression that had been with her since the death of their last son.

World Travelers

The Pierces left Washington in late spring of 1857 and went back to New Hampshire. In the fall, they decided to go abroad. When he learned of their proposed trip, President Buchanan offered the Pierces the use of the government ship *Powhatan*. After wintering in Madeira (a Portuguese island in the Atlantic Ocean), they went on to tour Europe. They visited Portugal, Spain, France, Switzerland, Italy, Austria, Germany, Belgium, and England. They spent the summer of 1858 on the shores of Lake Geneva in Switzerland and the winter in Italy, where the Pierces had a happy reunion with Nathaniel Hawthorne in Rome. Hawthorne, seeing Pierce's white hair and lined face, noted that his friend had changed. He thought the presidency had taken a lot out of Pierce.

While they were in Europe, Pierce read all the political news he could find about the United States. Former Cabinet members wrote him occasionally, keeping him informed about fraud in Buchanan's administration and other troubles. In a way, it made Pierce feel better to learn that Buchanan was not doing much better than he had done in the presidency. But on the other hand, it was sad to be away and watch his beloved country tearing itself apart. Homesick for America, the Pierces returned to Boston in the summer of 1859. They had traveled a great deal and seen a lot, but it had not changed Jane's sorrowful manner much. She still dwelt in the sad past with her "precious dead sons."

A SERIOUS PROBLEM

It had been nearly three years since Pierce was President, and once again it was election time. The Democrats were looking for a man who could unite the country. There was growing tension between the North and South, and more fighting than there had been in 1857, when Pierce had left for Europe.

The Dred Scott decision of the U.S. Supreme Court had angered northern abolitionists. According to this decision, black slaves were not citizens, nor was a slave who had temporarily lived in a free state a free person. It further stated that the Missouri Compromise of 1820, which had outlawed slavery in the territories, was unconstitutional. Pierce had always maintained the same thing, which made many southerners begin to think about Pierce for President again.

More Violence in Kansas

Because of the two groups of armed men in Kansas, one upholding slavery and the other determined to abolish it, trouble continued in the territory. The constitution drawn up by Kansas at Lecompton, which guaranteed the right to own slaves in Kansas, was voted down by a large margin. President Buchanan declared the vote illegal and submitted the constitution to Congress. This caused an open breach between free and slave groups in Congress. When the Lecompton Constitution was again submitted to the people of Kansas by the federal government, they voted to remain territorial citizens rather than be a divided state.

Violence ended in Kansas, but the slavery issue did not go away. Republican Abraham Lincoln and Democrat Stephen A. Douglas held several debates on the issues of slavery and Kansas in 1858, and it eventually became clear that sooner or later America would have to accept slavery everywhere in the United States or totally reject it.

Then, in the fall of 1859, came abolitionist John Brown's raid on Harper's Ferry, Virginia, followed by his capture, trial, and execution. Pierce thought that Brown was a fanatic, trying to use force to destroy the whole country. He restated his position that slavery was constitutional and that the North would have to live with it. Several southerners who admired Pierce suggested to him privately in Boston that he run for the presidency in 1860. Pierce declined, and he meant it. He vowed never to become part of national politics again.

The Democratic Party Splits

Franklin Pierce had bought 60 acres of land on Pleasant Street in Concord but delayed building a home on the property. For Jane, there were too many memories of Benjamin in Concord. When they returned from Europe, the Pierces decided to live in Concord only occasionally.

But the harsh New Hampshire winters were not good for Jane's health, and the Pierces went to the West Indies. While preparing to leave, the former President was asked who he thought was the best Democratic candidate for President, and he said, "Jefferson Davis." Davis had been a loyal secretary of war, and to Pierce's mind he was the one to unite the northern and southern wings of the party.

After wintering in the West Indies, Pierce and Jane returned home in June to find that the Democratic Party for which Pierce had worked so hard for so long had split. The national convention had broken up without nominating a candidate for President.

Caleb Cushing and other old friends tried to convince Pierce that he must be the Democratic candidate in order to bring the warring factions of the party together again. Pierce declined in a strong letter, saying that he was not a leader of forlorn hopes and that he had suffered enough in the presidency. Had he wanted to be President again, he told them, he would still have refused, as his beloved Jane was very ill. If she even heard about the possibility of returning to Washington, it would destroy her completely. Pierce was finished with national politics, but he was still concerned about preserving the Union.

Even before the election of 1860, the Democrats knew

they would be defeated by Republican candidate Abraham Lincoln because of the split in their party. They now had two tickets. Stephen A. Douglas, the candidate of the moderates and Free-Soil men headed one, and John Breckinridge, the candidate of the South, headed the other. It was late, but people were still asking Pierce to be a compromise candidate. They argued that if he let them use his name, perhaps the other two candidates would withdraw, but Pierce refused. He liked the idea of a compromise candidate, though, and he suggested James Guthrie, his former secretary of the treasury. However, the party ignored his suggestion.

THE SOUTH SECEDES FROM THE UNION

Following Abraham Lincoln's election as President in 1860, the southern states put in motion their plans to secede (withdraw) from the Union. Friends pleaded with Pierce, whom they thought had influence over the southerners, to persuade them to stay. But he still believed, as the South did, that slavery was guaranteed under the states' rights provision of the Constitution and could not be interfered with legally. However, Pierce did ask the North to be gentle with the South. He did not realize that antisouthern feelings in the North were very strong.

Then news came of the secession of South Carolina and of conventions to be held in other southern states to secede from the Union. The federal government planned to send commissioners to each of those states. Friends wanted Pierce to become a commissioner to Alabama, but he was not feeling well. Instead, he wrote a letter asking southerners to stay in the Union and to remember that they had many friends in the North who had always defended their rights. But his letter did not carry any more weight than did his appeal to northerners to treat the South gently. Antinorthern feelings in the South were also very strong.

Shots at Fort Sumter

When South Carolina cut off supplies to Fort Sumter, in the harbor at Charleston, President Buchanan sent a ship to the fort to bring provisions. Pierce wrote, "I cannot conceive of a more idle, foolish, ill-advised, if not criminal thing." The action, he said, would certainly mean war.

Former President John Tyler was in Washington for a peace conference, and it was suggested that all the former Presidents meet there. But at the time, Pierce did not agree. He was still ill. Also, he could see no point in a conference given the views of extremists on both sides, who, in his opinion, were bent on civil war. He believed the northerners had taken the first wrong step, and no appeal could be made to the South unless the North gave up its position.

Lincoln was inaugurated on March 4, 1861. On April 12, when Confederate guns fired on Fort Sumter, the Civil War began. Pierce immediately declared his loyalty to the Union, and at the same time he reconsidered the idea of a meeting of former Presidents. He wrote Martin Van Buren, the oldest living former President, suggesting that he call a meeting at Philadelphia to show unity. It would have been a promising group of men: John Tyler, Millard Fillmore, Martin Van Buren, Pierce, and James Buchanan. But Van Buren refused and suggested that Pierce do it. Nothing was done.

Opposing the War

Pierce was against the war and gave a speech criticizing the administration. During the summer of 1861, he visited friends in Michigan and Kentucky and made a few more speeches. On Christmas Eve, Pierce was at Andover, New Hampshire, when he received a letter from Secretary of State William H. Seward in which Seward enclosed a copy of a letter that had been sent to him by a Michigan postmaster. It said that "General P----" had just taken a trip to help an antiwar organization (Knights of the Golden Circle) that was going to overthrow the government. Seward wrote an insulting letter to Pierce practically accusing him of treason.

Pierce was furious. True, he had spoken out against the war, but it was not even close to treason. He answered Seward with an indignant letter in which he said, "It is not easy to conceive how any person [could believe] . . . that I am connected . . . with any league to overthrow the Government of my country." Pierce was bitter; he had served as President and struggled for four years to maintain the Union.

Although Seward promptly apologized and Pierce thought it would end the matter, excerpts from the same letter kept showing up in newspapers. Pierce asked Senator Milton Latham of California to bring the matter before the Senate. An investigation revealed that the letter was a hoax. Although he was cleared, Franklin Pierce never regained the position of respect given to former Presidents, and as the war continued, he became increasingly bitter.

When Lincoln issued the Emancipation Proclamation, which freed the slaves, Pierce condemned it. He declared that the real purpose of the war was to overthrow the Constitution. He could not understand why the people of his country wanted to "butcher" their race in order to "inflict" freedom on four million blacks, who were "in no way capable of profiting by freedom."

But bitter as he was against Lincoln's administration, Pierce felt the South had committed a sin by destroying the Union. On July 4, 1863, at Concord, Franklin Pierce made a strong speech attacking the President and calling the war this "fearful, fruitless, fatal civil war." The speech alienated so many people that his last shred of reputation was destroyed. Pierce was never again thought of as a great statesman in New Hampshire or the nation.

LAST YEARS

In the next six years, there were many signs that Franklin Pierce was losing his spirit and power. To add to his personal troubles, his beloved Jane died on December 2, 1863. Hawthorne was at the funeral to comfort his friend, but died himself soon after, in the spring of 1864. Because of Pierce's reputation as a traitor, he was not included as a pallbearer at Hawthorne's funeral, although they had been the best of friends.

Pierce was alone now. He had lost his wife and his best friend. Numb with grief, the former President retired to his home in Concord. Then, as the Civil War drew to a close, it brought one more final blow.

It was 1864 – election time again. The Republicans unearthed some letters Pierce had written to Jefferson Davis years before. In addition, Pierce's actions in Kansas were viewed as an attempt to make Kansas a slave state. Because Davis was now president of the Confederacy, the charges that Pierce had been a traitor seemed to be true, particularly to the young people who had been children during the years when Pierce was President. These accusations almost destroyed Pierce and the Democratic Party. From then on, Pierce kept a low profile in Concord, except for urging a few Democrats to support General George McClellan as their presidential candidate. The party did – but McClellan lost to Lincoln.

Then, tragically, President Lincoln was assassinated, and the angry mob appeared at Pierce's house. So, the last years were unhappy ones for Franklin Pierce. Union soldiers never forgot his opposition to the Civil War, but they did forget his support of war charities and his concern for the men who fought. Frequently ill, he was often alone, and in his loneliness, began to drink again. He objected to the sermons at the South Congregationalist Church, which railed against the sin of slavery and advocated punishing the South. Because Pierce was not getting any feeling of peace from being a Congregationalist, he became an Episcopalian.

A Time for Mourning

To keep busy, Pierce bought 84 acres of land at Little Boar's Head on the New Hampshire coast and built a cottage there. He planned a summer colony development, too. Pierce spent summers at Little Boar's Head and while there in 1869, he became very ill. It took all his strength to return to Concord in September, when he moved into the home of Willard Williams. Pierce was now 64 years old. During the next few weeks, his illness became worse, and soon he could no longer get out of bed. Drifting in and out of consciousness, Franklin Pierce died just before dawn on Friday morning, October 8, 1869.

President Grant ordered a period of national mourning, and Pierce's body was taken to the state capitol, where the townspeople paid their respects. Stores were closed for an hour at noon on Monday, the day of the funeral, and schools were dismissed so children could watch the procession. After the funeral ceremony at St. Paul's Episcopal Church, Pierce was buried in Concord's Old North Cemetery. The governor of New Hampshire and the mayor of Concord were among the pallbearers.

Because he stood for states' rights on the eve of the Civil War, New Hampshiremen refused for years to honor the memory of Franklin Pierce. Finally, in 1895 former U.S. Senator William E. Chandler persuaded the people of the Granite State that they owed a debt of gratitude to the President who fought so hard to preserve the Union. A memorial project was organized. But because there was still so much opposition to Pierce, it was not until 1913 that the state legislature voted funds for the project. Then, in 1914, a memorial statue was erected in front of the post office, near the statehouse.

LOOKING BACK

In the years that followed Pierce's death, historians called him one of the weaker American Presidents, with an administration that often swung indecisively from one course of action to another. For the most part, Pierce had selected poor advisors, and he conducted presidential affairs not as a leader, but as a member of his own Cabinet. Trying to protect the values of the framers of the Constitution, he and his associates saw no need for new concepts or for a more complex set of values.

President Harry Truman listed Pierce as one of the eight worst Presidents, declaring that he made a mess of things because he was a northerner who believed in slavery. Truman said, "He left few writings or deeds that have been long remembered, and no high accomplishments. His administrative talents were limited and his grasp of international situations lacking."

However, in all fairness, Franklin Pierce should be measured against his own time. With the North and South moving toward what was later called "the irrepressible conflict" over slavery, so much was happening that Pierce had all he could do to hold the country together. As a New Hampshireman who had no slaves, the small-town country lawyer suffered greatly for his conviction that slavery was constitutional.

But Franklin Pierce brought to the presidency a certain dignity and a concern for the basic rights of people. As President, he had to battle a difficult combination of inner turmoil, personal tragedy, and national confusion—all of which probably kept him from becoming a better leader.

Bibliography

Hoyt, Edwin P. *Franklin Pierce: The Fourteenth President of the United States.* New York: Abelard-Schuman, 1972. An interesting 148-page biography of Pierce and his times written for young people. It is amply illustrated and fun to read.

Kane, Joseph Nathan. *Facts About the Presidents.* New York: H.W. Wilson, 1959. A large volume that includes comparative as well as biographical data about the presidents.

Minor, Henry. *The Story of the Democratic Party.* New York: Macmillan, 1928. This book traces the beginnings of the Democratic Party and follows it through many ups and downs. It will help in understanding party loyalty and why Franklin Pierce was a dedicated Democrat.

Nichols, Roy Franklin. *Franklin Pierce: Young Hickory of the Granite Hills.* Philadelphia: University of Pennsylvania Press, 1931; revised 1958. A detailed, full-length biography of Pierce—the only one available—complete with notes.

Wallace, Edward S. *Destiny and Glory.* New York: Coward-McCann, 1957. A popular account of the adventures of various groups of Americans (filibusters) who made hostile expeditions to the Caribbean islands and to Central and South America during the years between the Mexican-American War and Civil War.

Index